The Changing
Roles of Debt
and Equity
in Financing U.S.
Capital Formation

A Project Report
National Bureau of
Economic Research

The Changing Roles of Debt and Equity in Financing U.S. Capital Formation

Edited by Benjamin M. Friedman

The University of Chicago Press

Chicago and London

Benjamin M. Friedman is Professor of Economics at Harvard University and Program Director for Financial Markets and Monetary Economics at the National Bureau of Economic Research.

The University of Chicago Press, Chicago 60637
The University of Chicago Press, Ltd., London
© 1982 by The National Bureau of Economic Research
All rights reserved. Published 1982
Printed in the United States of America
89 88 87 86 85 84 83   5 4 3 2

Library of Congress Cataloging in Publication Data
Main entry under title:

The Changing roles of debt and equity in financing U.S.
  capital formation

(A Project report/National Bureau of Economic
Research)
  Based on papers presented at a conference held in
Williamsburg, Va., Apr. 2–3, 1981, sponsored by the
National Bureau of Economic Research.
  Includes bibliographies and index.
  1. Saving and investment—United States—Congresses.
2. Capital market—United States—Congresses.
3. Corporations—United States—Finance—Congresses.
I. Friedman, Benjamin M.   II. National Bureau of Economic
Research.   III. Series: Project Report (National Bureau
of Economic Research)
HG4910.C49   332'.0415'0973   81-16353
ISBN 0-226-26340-1   AACR2

82–12360

Relation of the Directors to the
Work and Publications of the
National Bureau of Economic Research

1. The object of the National Bureau of Economic Research is to ascertain and to present to the public important economic facts and their interpretation in a scientific and impartial manner. The Board of Directors is charged with the reponsibility of ensuring that the work of the National Bureau is carried on in strict conformity with this object.

2. The President of the National Bureau shall submit to the Board of Directors, or to its Executive Committee, for their formal adoption all specific proposals for research to be instituted.

3. No research report shall be published by the National Bureau until the President has sent each member of the Board a notice that a manuscript is recommended for publication and that in the President's opinion it is suitable for publication in accordance with the principles of the National Bureau. Such notification will include an abstract or summary of the manuscript's content and a response form for use by those Directors who desire a copy of the manuscript for review. Each manuscript shall contain a summary drawing attention to the nature and treatment of the problem studied, the character of the data and their utilization in the report, and the main conclusions reached.

4. For each manuscript so submitted, a special committee of the Directors (including Directors Emeriti) shall be appointed by majority agreement of the President and Vice Presidents (or by the Executive Committee in case of inability to decide on the part of the President and Vice Presidents), consisting of three Directors selected as nearly as may be one from each general division of the Board. The names of the special manuscript committee shall be stated to each Director when notice of the proposed publication is submitted to him. It shall be the duty of each member of the special manuscript committee to read the manuscript. If each member of the manuscript committee signifies his approval within thirty days of the transmittal of the manuscript, the report may be published. If at the end of that period any member of the manuscript committee withholds his approval, the President shall then notify each member of the Board, requesting approval or disapproval of publication, and thirty days additional shall be granted for this purpose. The manuscript shall then not be published unless at least a majority of the entire Board who shall have voted on the proposal within the time fixed for the receipt of votes shall have approved.

5. No manuscript may be published, though approved by each member of the special manuscript committee, until forty-five days have elapsed from the transmittal of the report in manuscript form. The interval is allowed for the receipt of any memorandum of dissent or reservation, together with a brief statement of his reasons, that any member may wish to express; and such memorandum of dissent or reservation shall be published with the manuscript if he so desires. Publication does not, however, imply that each member of the Board has read the manuscript, or that either members of the Board in general or the special committee have passed on its validity in every detail.

6. Publications of the National Bureau issued for informational purposes concerning the work of the Bureau and its staff, or issued to inform the public of activities of Bureau staff, and volumes issued as a result of various conferences involving the National Bureau shall contain a specific disclaimer noting that such publication has not passed through the normal review procedures required in this resolution. The Executive Committee of the Board is charged with review of all such publications from time to time to ensure that they do not take on the character of formal research reports of the National Bureau, requiring formal Board approval.

7. Unless otherwise determined by the Board or exempted by the terms of paragraph 6, a copy of this resolution shall be printed in each National Bureau publication.

(Resolution adopted October 25, 1926, as revised through September 30, 1974)

Contents

Acknowledgments

This volume, consisting of papers presented at a conference held at Williamsburg, Va., 2–3 April 1981, is a progress report on the National Bureau of Economic Research project, The Changing Roles of Debt and Equity in Financing U.S. Capital Formation. The National Bureau has undertaken this project—including the conference, the research described in this volume, and the publication of the volume itself—with the support of the American Council of Life Insurance.

The many people whose advice and assistance have helped to make this volume possible include National Bureau directors George T. Conklin, Jr., Robert C. Holland, and Eli Shapiro; National Bureau research associates David F. Bradford, Robert J. Shiller, and Lawrence H. Summers; National Bureau staff members Mark Fitz-Patrick, Kirsten Foss, Lawrence McFaddin, Cynthia Nelson, and Annie Spillane; J. Robert Ferrari of the Prudential Insurance Company; Francis H. Schott of the Equitable Life Assurance Society; and Kenneth M. Wright of the American Council of Life Insurance.

The opinions expressed in this volume are those of the respective authors. They do not necessarily reflect the views of the National Bureau of Economic Research, the American Council of Life Insurance, or any other organization.

Benjamin M. Friedman

Introduction: An Overview of the NBER's Research Project on The Changing Roles of Debt and Equity in Financing U.S. Capital Formation

Benjamin M. Friedman

With the approach of the 1980s, the National Bureau of Economic Research identified the issue of capital formation as a primary target for empirical economic research. Several considerations made this choice a sensible one. Economic thinking has nearly always emphasized the central role of fixed capital in the physical production process. In addition, the evolution of public policy discussion in the United States during the 1970s had made clear that economists and business leaders were not alone in calling for an increased rate of capital formation. What may once have been an esoteric subject had emerged as a widely supported national objective. Finally—and most importantly, from the National Bureau's perspective—the nature of many of the important questions involved in the capital formation issue suggested the potential ability of serious empirical economic research to increase basic understanding.

Within the National Bureau's overall research effort, questions about capital formation also seemed to represent a natural direction for the Financial Markets and Monetary Economics program. In an advanced economy like that of the United States, with highly developed financial markets, capital formation represents not just the allocation of physical resources but the allocation of financial resources as well. Every physical investment decision has its financial counterpart. Moreover, a large body of evidence indicates that these financial allocations do not simply mirror corresponding physical allocations that would take place in any case. The financial and the physical aspects of businesses' and individuals' decisions in this area are fully interdependent, so that the surrounding financial environment importantly affects both the amount and the composition of the capital formation that the economy as a whole undertakes.

Indeed, financial influences on capital formation in the American economy are so many and so pervasive that some more specific focus was necessary for even a major research project. In this context the respective roles of debt and equity in financing capital formation stood out as being of particular interest, at least in part because these roles not only appear to have been undergoing some change but also seem likely to evolve further in the future. Hence the choice of specific subject: The Changing Roles of Debt and Equity in Financing U.S. Capital Formation.

The starting point for this research effort was a pair of broad questions about the markets in which the debt and equity securities of business corporations undertaking physical capital formation are issued, traded, and priced. First, how have the markets priced corporate debt and equity securities in the past, and what aspects of the markets' functioning have accounted for these evaluations? Second, how have corporations' financing patterns responded in this environment, and what specific aspects of the interaction between the market mechanism and corporate financing decisions have accounted for these responses? Fourteen papers addressing these questions, written by eighteen National Bureau researchers, constituted the first major stage of the project.

The papers in this volume are the authors' summaries of six of these fourteen papers. These six papers were prepared for a conference that the National Bureau sponsored at Williamsburg, Va. on 2–3 April 1981. The conference provided an opportunity to report on this research to, and receive valuable feedback from, an audience consisting of financial market practitioners representing investment management firms, insurance companies, commercial banks, and investment banking firms, as well as financial officers of corporations in nonfinancial lines of business. The six papers presented at that conference, and published here for the first time, provide a balanced overview of the first major stage of this research project, which is now complete.

How Have the Markets Priced Corporate Debt and Equity Securities?

The majority of the papers prepared during the first stage of the research project adopted a market perspective. Two of these papers examined the historical experience directly. Three focused on the core of the market mechanism consisting of the relationships connecting expectations, risk, and market prices. Four additional papers addressed specific questions including inflation risk, the interaction between inflation and market regulation, effects of federal debt management policy, and the increasing internationalization of the U.S. financial markets.

Patric H. Hendershott, in his paper "Inflation, Resource Utilization, and Debt and Equity Returns," reviewed the basic pricing experience in the U.S. debt and equity markets during the past half-century. More specifically, Hendershott investigated the relationships among Treasury bill rates, the realized returns on Treasury bonds and bills, and the realized returns on equities and corporate bonds, in the context of variations in price inflation as well as the business cycle. His analysis therefore provided a background for considering the fundamental portfolio decision concerning the broad division of investable funds among equities, long-term debt, and short-term debt.

Hendershott's analysis documented three separate findings. First, the experience of real and nominal returns on Treasury bills since the 1951 Treasury–Federal Reserve Accord has differed sharply from the corresponding pre-Accord patterns. In earlier years nominal bill yields were reasonably stable and real yields extremely volatile, while more recently the nominal bill rate has cycled around a rising trend and real rates have stayed near zero. Second, unanticipated changes in bond coupon yields have dominated the relative return relationship between bonds and Treasury bills. Because bond coupon rates have risen with (unexpected) inflation during the past fifteen years, bonds have earned negative real returns. Third, the relative return relationship between bonds and equities has varied systematically over the business cycle, with equities earning large positive relative returns around business cycle troughs and large negative relative returns around peaks.

Hendershott's paper, which appears as Chapter 1 of this volume, is an introduction to a more comprehensive study which will be part of the second stage of this overall research project.

William C. Brainard, John B. Shoven, and Lawrence Weiss, in their paper "The Financial Valuation of the Return to Capital" (*Brookings Papers on Economic Activity* No. 2, 1980), also examined the market's valuation of equities and other claims to corporate capital. They used cross-section data on the valuation of a sample of U.S. firms at different times to estimate the time-discount and risk-adjustment factors necessary to explain the observed market values for these firms during the twenty years 1958–77. Cross-sectional variation in the relevant measures of the riskiness of earnings streams having the same time profile of expected returns provided the means by which they could distinguish separate time-discount and risk-adjustment factors.

The method used by Brainard, et al., to calculate the present discounted value of future cash flows for each firm in each year involved first calculating the age structure, replacement value, and rate of return of the firm's capital stock. They then computed aggregate series of gross and net returns. Finally, to explore the sensitivity of their results to variations in assumptions about expectation formation, they used ten different methods of forecasting future earnings.

The results of this analysis confirmed a large decline in market values relative to the present values of after-tax cash flows, discounted by either a constant real rate or an inflation-adjusted bond rate. Specifically, the real discount rate required to equate market and present discounted values increased from less than five percent in the late 1960s to more than ten percent on average in the late 1970s. Moreover, these results did not depend on a particular, perhaps overly optimistic, assumption about expected future earnings. The sharp decline in firms' market values relative to present values of the corresponding streams emerged even with the most pessimistic of the ten earnings expectations models, which assumed a continuation of the historically low rates of return experienced in the latter part of the sample period.

Brainard, et al., also briefly considered four familiar factors sometimes hypothesized to account for this decline in valuation: increased investor aversion to risk; an increased tax burden on corporate earnings due to price inflation; investors' inability to assess earnings streams correctly because of inflation; and an overall decrease in expected rates of return due to higher energy prices and/or increased government regulation. The results along these lines were mixed at best. In the end the authors concluded that the combination of measurable characteristics of firms and conventional methods of projecting and discounting future earnings is not likely to explain the decline in market values that dominated the 1970s.

Robert C. Merton, in his paper "On Estimating the Expected Return on the Market: An Exploratory Investigation" (*Journal of Financial Economics*, December 1980), examined a series of issues relating to the measurement of expected returns assessed against their riskiness in the equity market. The expected return on "the market" is a concept often central to problems in both portfolio management and corporate finance. For example, to implement even the most passive investment strategy, an investor must have some idea of the expected return on the market in order to determine how much of his portfolio to allocate to a fully diversified mix of equity holdings. Similarly, the expected equity return is an important element in determining "hurdle rates" for capital budgeting, or the allowed "fair" rate of return in regulated industries.

The conventional way to estimate this expected return, at least for purposes of economic research, is to adjust the prevailing return on some "safe" alternative to equities—say, a short-term interest rate—according to the historical average difference by which equity returns have exceeded this alternative. This procedure does, of course, explicitly reflect the dependence of the expected equity return on prevailing interest rates. By contrast, it does not take into account the effect of changes in the level of risk associated with equities, or changes in investors' attitudes toward that risk. It is clear that the dependence of expected return on risk in this context could matter in principle. Merton's object was to evaluate whether in fact it matters importantly in practice.

Merton addressed this question by analyzing the implications of three models of securities pricing that explicitly reflect the dependence of the expected equity return on changing risk. In each case he derived a set of procedures for estimating the expected return on the market that incorporated the underlying pricing model, as well as the constraint that, as a consequence of risk aversion, the expected return on the market must exceed the return on riskless assets. Merton then estimated each of these three models using U.S. data for 1926–78.

The chief conclusion from this analysis was that the presence or absence of risk dependence, and its specific form if present, are both quantitatively important for the estimation of the expected market return. In other words, because the average variability of the realized market return changes significantly over time, it is important to allow for changes in the variability associated with expected market returns when predicting the expected return in the market in excess of "safe" alternatives.

Robert J. Shiller, in his paper "Do Stock Prices Move Too Much to Be Justified by Subsequent Changes in Dividends?" (*American Economic Review*, June 1981) examined from a different perspective the same question of the variability of equity prices and returns. The particular focus of Shiller's investigation was the combination of the "dividend discount" relationship between equity prices and expected future dividends and the "efficient markets" principle that investors exploit all available information in anticipating the future. More specifically, the dividend discount model, stated in inflation-adjusted terms, asserts that real equity prices equal the real values of expected future real dividends discounted by the appropriate real interest rate; a particular version of this model, which has found substantial acceptance in practice, further assumes that the relevant real interest rate is constant or nearly so. The efficient markets principle in turn asserts that equity prices at any time already incorporate all available information about the future of dividends, so that changes in dividend expectations (and hence in equity prices) reflect only new information as it emerges.

Shiller's goal was to test the familiar objection that observed equity prices are too volatile to be consistent with a pricing mechanism based on the dividend discount model combined with the efficient markets principle. The point of this objection is simply that observed movements in real equity prices are too large, in comparison with the subsequently experienced movements in real dividends, to be realistically attributed to any objective flow of new information about those dividends. Hence either the dividend discount model or the efficient markets principle (or both) must be inadequate as a characterization of how the market works.

Shiller found that tests based on data for the Standard and Poor's Composite Stock Price Index since 1870, and for the Dow Jones Industrial Average since 1928, bear out this objection. More specifically, after adjustments for price inflation and a time trend, the observed movements in equity prices could have been justified as the rational response to new information about expected future dividend movements only if the latter were many times bigger than those actually observed. Alternatively, variation in the (unobserved) real interest rate could have reconciled the observed movements in equity prices and rationally expected future dividend movements only if that variation had been implausibly large. On the basis of these results, Shiller concluded that the combination of the dividend discount model and the efficient markets principle does not provide an adequate description of the equity market's pricing mechanism.

John G. Cragg and Burton G. Malkiel, in their paper "Expectations and the Valuation of Shares" (forthcoming as part of a National Bureau monograph bearing the same title), used data collected from a survey of financial analysts to explore the equity market pricing mechanism. During the 1960s Cragg and Malkiel had obtained estimates of the short- and long-run changes in individual company earnings, together with related financial information, from seventeen major investment firms. Their research had two main objectives: to characterize the surveyed expectations in relation to familiar theories of expectations like those encompassed in the efficient markets principle; and to examine the role of these expectations in the determination of the prices of individual companies' equities.

On the first question, Cragg and Malkiel found that the surveyed expectations failed in a number of ways to conform to the assumptions often made in efficient markets models. On the second question, however, they found that the surveyed expectations did seem to have affected equity prices, both in ways suggested by the familiar theory and in apparently other ways too. In particular, despite the familiar theoretical principle that the market takes account of only systematic (that is, market-related) risk in pricing a security, Cragg and Malkiel found, first, that a variety of systematic factors appear to affect security prices and, second, that specific (that is, market-independent) risk may also affect the price of a company's equities.

Malkiel's paper "Risk and Return: A New Look," which appears as Chapter 2 of this volume, summarizes and extends this work.

Zvi Bodie, in his paper "Innovation for Stable Real Retirement Income" (*Journal of Portfolio Management*, Fall 1980), addressed the problems that price inflation causes for all savers including in particular those saving for their retirement. Bodie showed that conventional U.S. debt and equity financial instruments—including short-term money market instruments, long-term bonds, and equities—have all failed to provide holders with an adequate hedge against inflation during the past twenty-five years. On average, money market instruments have borne a small positive after-inflation return and equities a larger return, while bonds have borne a negative after-inflation return. The returns on all three kinds of instruments have been highly volatile, however, both before and after inflation.

Bodie focused on finding the most appropriate asset base in the U.S. capital markets for funding price-indexed retirement savings plans. He found that, during the past twenty-five years, the investment strategy offering the least risky after-inflation rate of return would have been to hold money market instruments together with a small position in a well-diversified portfolio of commodity futures contracts. The after-inflation return that such a portfolio would have earned, however, is approximately zero. In more recent work, also done within this overall research project, Bodie has extended this analysis by considering the tradeoff between risk and return facing an investor in the U.S. capital markets who is concerned about after-inflation returns but is not solely interested in minimizing risk. Money market instruments are once again the cornerstone of any low-risk investment strategy, and equities are the main ingredient in any high-return portfolio. Commodity futures contracts are the only asset whose after-inflation return is positively correlated with inflation. Adding them to a portfolio therefore lowers the risk associated with any target after-inflation rate of return.

Bodie's paper "Investment Strategy in an Inflationary Environment," which appears as Chapter 3 of this volume, summarizes and extends this work.

Edward J. Kane, in his paper "Accelerating Inflation and the Distribution of Household Savings Incentives" (in *Stagflation: The Causes, Effects, and Solutions*, U.S. Congress, Joint Economic Committee, December 1980), used cross-section data to show how U.S. households in different economic and demographic classes have reallocated their savings in response to the combination of accelerating inflation and regulated deposit interest rates. On balance, these forces have led households of below-average wealth to shift their savings into tangible assets, especially real estate, and households of above-average wealth to shift their savings into unregulated financial assets. Both responses have increased the riskiness of savers' portfolios.

Kane's analysis showed how, both to hedge inflation risk on their nondiscretionary contractual savings and to eke out a positive net after-tax real return on their discretionary savings, all but the wealthiest U.S. households have found it advantageous to substitute investments in housing and other real estate, as well as consumer durables and collectibles, in place of traditional saving vehicles like deposit accounts and savings bonds. By contrast, as a result of differential taxes and transactions costs, the nation's wealthiest households have moved on balance out of both traditional deposit accounts and home equity into certificates of deposit, marketable bonds, and equity in investment real estate. Given these new riskier portfolios, less wealthy households have actually fared better than have wealthy households. Real returns earned by wealthy households have been poor, as bond prices have fallen and equity values have failed to keep pace with inflation, while trends in the relative price of housing have rewarded those who shifted heavily into real estate, especially on a highly leveraged basis.

Kane's analysis also revealed several other important trends, including a greatly increased emphasis on leveraged housing investment among young households and an increased concentration of marketable bonds and equities among wealthy households. Households headed by persons under age twenty-five have greatly expanded their equity in houses, although still not enough to lift the overall return on their savings up to the level achieved by older groups. The tendency to buy smaller homes, due to smaller family size as well as restricted financing opportunities, has held down young households' ability to earn comparable rates of return. The increasingly tight concentration of marketable securities in the hands of wealthy investors suggests that only they could economically engage in strictly financial-market disintermediation. It also explains regulators' strategy of relaxing deposit interest ceilings only on minimum-deposit (and longer-maturity) accounts.

These findings served to underscore the unintended consequences of the combination of accelerating inflation and deposit interest ceilings. The ultimate economic effects have been to distort the sectoral composition of saving and risk-bearing in ways likely to crowd out productive business investment, as well as to distort the distributions of income and opportunity.

V. Vance Roley, in his paper "The Effect of Federal Debt Management Policy on Corporate Bond and Equity Yields" (*Quarterly Journal of Economics*, in press), addressed the effect on U.S. debt and equity yields associated not with the government's overall deficit total but with its manner of financing that deficit. In theory, federal debt management policy may play an important role in determining the yield structure of both government and private securities. Previous empirical studies, however, have typically failed to detect quantitatively significant effects of federal debt management. By contrast, using a disaggregated structural model of the markets for government and private securities, Roley found that such effects were important.

The maturity composition of the federal debt has exhibited dramatic changes during the past thirty years. In 1950 the average maturity of the U.S. Treasury's outstanding debt held by private investors was 124 months. The average maturity fell steadily to 58 months in 1960, as the Treasury shifted to a greater reliance on short-term securities. Despite the "Operation Twist" policy of the early 1960s, the average maturity in fact remained stable during 1960–66, but thereafter it declined further to a low of 29 months in 1975, in large part because of the 4.25 percent interest ceiling on new Treasury bond issues. Beginning in 1975 the Treasury embarked on a policy to lengthen the federal debt, and as a result the average maturity rose to 46 months in 1980.

The impact of debt management policy on corporate debt and equity returns depends in the first instance on the degree of substitutability among government securities of different maturity, and on the substitutability between government securities and private securities, within investors' portfolios. It also depends on the responses of private debt and equity issuers. In one extreme, for example, the ultimate impact of a federal debt management operation could be an unchanged structure of yields together with a significant shift in the composition of corporate financing.

Roley's empirical results indicated that changes in the maturity composition of the federal debt significantly affect the markets for government and private securities, at least in the short run. In particular, the corporate bond yield closely follows the long-term government bond yield, while the equity yield shows smaller movements in the same direction. In the longer run the effects on yields are smaller than the initial impacts, even when the debt composition changes are permanent. In general, the results indicated that lengthening the federal debt reduces incentives for both bond and equity finance by the corporate sector, and vice versa.

David G. Hartman, in his paper "International Effects on the U.S. Capital Market" (NBER Working Paper No. 581), examined changes in the U.S. debt and equity markets due to the tendency toward greater economic interdependence. Hartman's principal finding was that the increasingly larger international capital flows have exerted significant effects on U.S. corporate bond rates. Moreover, since the corporate bond rate and other interest rates closely tied to it are often important determinants of physical investment decisions, this result suggests that international financial capital transactions also affect the U.S. rate of physical capital formation.

Hartman began by documenting the changing nature and magnitude of international transactions in the U.S. capital market. Although not long ago such transactions were small in comparison with the size of the U.S. market, in recent years foreign participation in the U.S. markets for both debt and equity securities has expanded greatly. Foreign investors are now major purchasers of both bonds and equities issued in the United States, and foreign borrowers now account for a significant fraction of all bonds issued in the United States. To date, foreign equity issues have been more limited.

Hartman then developed a model of the determination of the U.S. corporate bond rate that, in contrast to most interest rate models, admitted the possibility of international influences. Empirical evidence indicated that such influences are both significant and sizable.

How Has Corporate Financing Responded?

The remaining papers prepared during the first stage of the project shifted to the corporate perspective, focusing on the responses of corporations' financing to these market influences and on specific factors conditioning that response. One paper, which developed new historical data series from primary sources, examined the corporate financing and corporate balance sheet experience directly. Two papers addressed considerations associated with taxation in determining corporate financing decisions, one in the context of the differential tax treatment of dividends and capital gains, and one in the context of the risk of corporate bankruptcy. Two further papers addressed the rapid development of private pensions and the growth of the public debt through government deficits as specific external factors affecting corporate financing decisions, and highlighted the implications of these developments for U.S. capital formation.

John H. Ciccolo, Jr., in his paper "Changing Balance Sheet Relationships in the U.S. Manufacturing Sector, 1926–77," documented trends in the sources and uses of funds, market valuations, and rates of return for U.S. manufacturing firms during the half-century ending in 1977. The chief objective of Ciccolo's work was to derive economic balance sheet relationships based on market valuations of firms' securities rather than on the more familiar book values used for accounting purposes.

Among the more interesting long-term trends highlighted in Ciccolo's analysis is the finding that the widely recognized increase in debt in manufacturing firms' capitalization has come primarily at the expense of preferred stock. Relative to net assets, the market value of firms' debt plus preferred stock has remained virtually constant. A second interesting point is the contrast between the sharp fall in common equity values in 1929–32, which was entirely reversed by 1936, and the even sharper post-1968 decline which was not reversed even by 1977 (or, for that matter, 1981). Finally, although Ciccolo's work documented the long-term declining trend in dividend payments and the postwar rising trend in interest payments relative to firms' net assets, it showed that whether or not there has been a downward trend in the rate of return on either stockholders' equity or net assets depends largely on the beginning and ending dates chosen for the analysis.

Ciccolo's paper, which appears as Chapter 4 of this volume, is an introduction to a more comprehensive study which will be part of the second stage of this overall research project.

Roger H. Gordon and David F. Bradford, in their paper "Taxation and the Stock Market Valuation of Capital Gains and Dividends: Theory and Empirical Results" (*Journal of Public Economics*, October 1980), addressed the familiar puzzle of why U.S. corporations pay dividends. Because dividends appear to be more heavily taxed than capital gains, corporate shareholders ought to prefer either retained earnings or stock repurchases to dividend payments, all other things being equal. In 1976, however, corporations distributed in dividends $25 billion of a total $63 billion of profit net of taxes and interest. Either corporations are not acting in the best interest of their shareholders, or shareholders desire dividends sufficiently for other reasons to offset the tax effect.

Gordon and Bradford approached this question by developing and estimating a model of the relative value of dividends and capital gains in the U.S. equity market. For tax and other reasons, the taxpayer population will exhibit a distribution of differing preferences between returns in the form of dividends and returns in the form of capital gains. Individual corporations' shares will differ in the division of their total return between the two forms, and investors making portfolio decisions will take this division into account along with the corporation's risk structure. The market equilibrium therefore determines a single rate of exchange between dividends and capital gains. Although this exchange rate cannot be observed directly, it can be inferred from market data.

Gordon and Bradford's results indicated that the exchange rate between dividends and capital gains varies cyclically around an average value of approximately unity. In other words, the relative values of dividends and capital gains tend toward equality. These results are unsurprising from the perspective of corporations' choices of dividends versus retentions, but they are inconsistent with the view that shareholders value dividends and capital gains solely for their after-tax cash flow. Possible explanations for this shareholder behavior include the potential role of dividends as a signal of the corporation's future profitability, the existence of a frequently neglected class of shareholders for whom dividends are less heavily taxed than capital gains, or even an irrational sheer preference for dividends.

The cyclical variation in these results also has direct implications for corporate financing and capital formation. In general, a cyclically high value of dividends relative to capital gains will call forth not only a higher retention rate but also a shift from debt to equity finance. To the extent that the same measure also represents the value in the market of an additional dollar of corporate investment, a cyclically high relative value of dividends also indicates an incentive to increased physical investment.

Roger H. Gordon and Burton G. Malkiel, in their paper "Taxation and Corporate Finance" (forthcoming as part of a Brookings Institution book bearing the same title), addressed the distortions to U.S. corporate financing and investment decisions introduced by taxation when the possibility of costly bankruptcy exists. Gordon and Malkiel used both time series and cross-section data on variations in U.S. corporate debt-equity ratios to examine the implications of a model of corporate financing and investment that explicitly allows for the possibility and costs of bankruptcy. Using data from actual bankruptcy experiences, they also estimated the magnitude of the efficiency costs associated with the distortions due to the existing tax structure, as well as the efficiency implications of several possible modifications of that structure.

Gordon and Malkiel's results indicated that, as long as corporations behave competitively, explicit allowance for bankruptcy costs is essential to explaining the observed corporate financial structure. Otherwise the theory leads to conclusions with clear counterfactual implications. The historical experience in the United States since World War II involved steadily increasing debt-equity ratios on balance until 1974. Their theory explains this pattern in terms of increasing inflation and interest rates together with increasing optimism about the future prospects of the corporate sector until the early 1970s. The greater instability of the economy during the mid-1970s apparently altered firms' assessments of possible bankruptcy costs, however, and debt ratios were slightly reduced after 1974.

Gordon and Malkiel's results also indicated that at least some of the distortions associated with the existing tax structure are quantitatively important. They estimated that the efficiency costs arising from tax incentives to increase debt-equity ratios are on the order of $3 billion per year, or about ten percent of corporate tax payments. By contrast, they found that the efficiency costs of distortions in the allocation of capital between the corporate and noncorporate sectors may be less important, especially in comparison with previous estimates using earlier models. In particular, their estimate of these costs is only one-fourth to one-third as large as previous estimates. Primarily as a result of the larger efficiency costs of distortions affecting debt-equity financing decisions, any of several changes in the tax structure aimed at lessening financing distortions in favor of debt would offer significant efficiency gains.

Martin Feldstein and Stephanie Seligman, in their paper "Pension Funding, Share Price, and National Saving" (*Journal of Finance*, in press), examined the effects of unfunded pension obligations on corporate share prices and explored the implications of these effects for national saving, the decline of the equity market in recent years, and the rationality of corporate financial behavior. Their analysis was based on information about inflation-adjusted income and assets for nearly two hundred large U.S. manufacturing firms.

Feldstein and Seligman found that corporate share prices fully reflect the conventional accounting measure of unfunded pension obligations.

The most important implication of this share price response is that the existence of unfunded pension liabilities does not necessarily entail a reduction in total private saving. Because the pension liability reduces the equity value of the firm, shareholders are given notice of its existence and hence an incentive to save more themselves. Unfunded private pensions therefore differ fundamentally from unfunded government-sponsored pensions like Social Security and civil service and military pensions.

Feldstein's paper "Private Pensions as Corporate Debt," which appears as Chapter 5 of this volume, summarizes and extends this work.

Finally, in my own paper, "The Relative Stability of Money and Credit 'Velocities' in the United States: Evidence and Some Speculations" (NBER Working Paper No. 645), I documented a long-standing stability in the relationship between outstanding debt and economic activity in the United States, and explored the implications for capital formation of several hypotheses that could explain this observed phenomenon. In particular, I showed that the aggregate of outstanding credit liabilities of all nonfinancial borrowers in the United States bears as close a relationship to U.S. nonfinancial activity as do the more familiar asset aggregates like the money stock (however measured) or the monetary base. This stability in the debt-to-income relationship reflects the net outcome of pronounced but offsetting movements of the public and private components of the total debt aggregate.

I suggested three different hypotheses that provide potential explanations for this phenomenon. Two of these hypotheses, one emphasizing taxpayers' actions and one based on credit market borrowing constraints, carry the implication that increases in government debt outstanding associated with financing budget deficits crowd out private financing and hence private capital formation. The third hypothesis, which emphasizes the portfolio preferences of lenders, implies that increased government financing will not crowd out private capital formation but will cause the private sector to shift from debt to equity financing.

My paper "Debt and Economic Activity in the United States," which appears as Chapter 6 of this volume, summarizes and extends this work.

1 Inflation, Resource Utilization, and Debt and Equity Returns

Patric H. Hendershott

1.1 Introduction

During the past half-century, the American economy has been subjected to numerous shocks. The greatest of these were the Depression and World War II, but there were also other wars, OPEC, and "regular" business cycles. As a result, both resource utilization and inflation have varied widely, and enormously diverse real and nominal ex post returns on equity and short- and long-term debt securities have accompanied these variations.

This chapter contains an examination of the relationships among these security returns and an analysis of the effects of inflation and resource utilization on the relationships. More specifically, I will report on the impact of inflation on Treasury bill rates; the realized returns on Treasury bonds versus bills; and realized returns on equities versus corporate bonds. Further, I will discuss the relationship between the business cycle and realized returns on equities versus bonds. Thus, the analysis provides a background for the fundamental portfolio decision regarding the broad division of investable funds into equities, long-term debt, and short-term debt.

Before turning to the analysis, a few words about the data are in order. First, all of the underlying yield data—equities, corporate bonds, Treasury bonds, and Treasury bills—are those compiled by Ibbotson and Sinquefield (1979, 1980). These are roughly representative of returns on

Patric H. Hendershott is Professor of Finance at the Ohio State University, where he holds the John W. Galbreath Chair in Real Estate, and research associate of the National Bureau of Economic Research.

This chapter is based upon a larger, ongoing study by Roger D. Huang and the author (1983). The underlying study provides econometric support for many of the propositions advanced here.

economy-wide "market" portfolios and are available monthly for the 1926–78 period. Second, these yields are realized, rather than expected, returns, except for those on Treasury bills which are both expected and realized because their one-month maturity equals the period over which the returns are calculated. Third, the returns—income plus capital gains (except for bills)—are before-tax returns. They are not truly representative of what either highly taxed or tax-exempt investors actually earned after tax (both investor groups presumably would have opted for portfolios with relative income and capital gains components different from the market average, and the former group, of course, paid taxes). Hopefully, differential returns, at least, are roughly representative of those earned by most investors.

1.2   Inflation and Treasury Bill Returns

During the 1926–80 period there was a single episode of significant deflation, 1930–32. In those three years the inflation rate ranged from −6 to −10 percent. Modest deflation also occurred in 1926–27, 1938, and 1949. In contrast, there have been three significant bursts of inflation—the beginning of World War II (9 percent in 1941 and 1942), the postwar surge (18 percent in 1946 and 9 percent in 1947) and the Korean War scare (6 percent in 1950 and 1951)—and the prolonged post-1967 inflationary era. The current inflation has ranged from slightly over 4 percent (adjusting for the impact of price controls in 1971–72) to double-digit inflation in 1974 and again in 1979–80.

The above overview of the 1926–80 period suggests that division of these years into four subperiods might be useful. These are 1926–1940 (which includes the Depression and all years of even modest deflation except 1949), 1941–51 (which includes the inflationary spurts of World War II, its aftermath, and the outbreak of the Korean conflict), 1952–67 (the era of stable prices), and 1968–80 (the present inflationary period). The first two columns of Table 1.1 present the mean and standard deviations for the annual inflation rate for these and overlapping periods. The great differences in the mean inflation rate and its variability are obvious.

The next four columns list means and standard deviations for both the nominal and real one-month Treasury bill rate.[1] As can be seen, there is

1. Data for nominal bill rates in 1979 and 1980 have been computed from the one-month tax-adjusted bill rates calculated by Huston McCulloch, whom I thank for making them available to me. To check the comparability of these rates with those of Ibbotson and Sinquefield, I computed the annual return on one-month bills in 1978 from McCulloch's data, 7.23 percent, and found that it differed little from that based on the I-S data, 7.18 percent. The method for calculating tax-adjusted yields is presented in J. Huston McCulloch (1975).

Table 1.1   Annual Inflation and Nominal and Real One-Month Treasury Bill Rates

	Inflation Rate		Nominal Bill Rate		Real Bill Rate	
	Mean	Std. Dev.	Mean	Std. Dev.	Mean	Std. Dev.
1926–40	−1.5	4.0	1.3	1.5	2.8	4.5
1941–51	6.0	5.3	0.6	0.4	−5.4	5.5
1952–67	1.5	1.2	2.7	1.0	1.2	0.8
1968–80	7.1	3.1	6.7	2.2	−0.4	1.8
1926–51	1.7	5.9	1.0	1.2	−0.6	6.4
1952–80	4.0	3.6	4.5	2.6	0.5	1.5

SOURCES: The inflation rate is the rate of change in the consumer price index for the 1926–46 period and the rate of change in the consumer price index net of the shelter component (to exclude the impact of changes in mortgage rates) after 1946. The nominal bill rate is from Ibbotson and Sinquefield (1980) for 1926–78 and McCulloch (1975) for 1979–80. The real rate is the nominal rate less the inflation rate. Annual rates are geometric averages of the twelve monthly rates during calendar years.

an enormous difference in the variability of the real bill rate between 1926–51 and 1952–80. In the latter period the standard deviation of the real bill rate, 1.5 percent, is only three-fifths of that of the nominal bill rate, 2.6 percent; in the earlier period the former, 6.4 percent, is over five times the latter, 1.2 percent. Division of the earlier interval into 1926–40 and 1941–51 reveals enormous variability in the real bill rate (and stability in the nominal rate). The mean real bill was a full 2.8 percent in 1926–40 and an incredible −5.4 percent in 1941–51. The negative real rate in the 1940s was due to the monetary authorities' policy of pegging nominal interest rates at low levels during a period of significant inflation. The high real rate in the 1930s is largely attributable to the combination of the general nonnegativity constraint on the nominal rate and the existence of significant deflation. However, it is noteworthy that the real bill rate exceeded 4 percent in all years in the 1926–30 period during which the nonnegativity constraint was not binding (the nominal bill rate ranged from 2.4 to 4.7 percent).

Figure 1.1 illustrates the marked difference between the 1926–51 and 1952–80 periods in the volatility of both the nominal and real bill rates. In the former period the nominal rate declines in the early 1930s and is then flat; in the latter period this rate cycles around a sharply rising trend (the 1980 average bill rate of almost 12 percent disguises variations in monthly rates between less than 7 percent and over 16 percent). In contrast, the real bill rate varied between +12 percent in 1931 and 1932 and −18 percent in 1946. Its often-cited stability clearly refers to the post-1951 period only.

Even the reduced variability of the real bill rate in the 1952–80 period (+2.5 to −4.5 percent) is possibly an overstatement of future variability because the sharply negative rates of 1973 and especially 1974 are un-

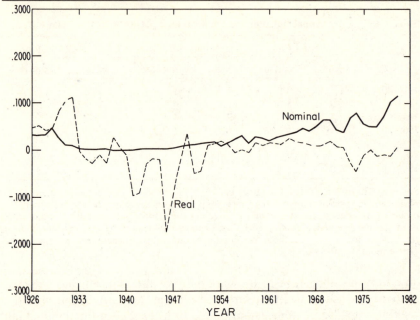

Fig. 1.1   Real and Nominal Treasury Bill Rates, 1926–80.

likely to recur.[2] Short-term bill rates became "out of line" relative to short-term rates on large CDs, commercial paper, and bankers acceptances in 1973, and especially 1974. To illustrate, the spread between yields on six-month CDs and bills increased in 1974 relative to normal years by about 110 basis points, and the spread between yields on three-month maturities jumped by 155 basis points. According to Cook (1981), the bill market was segmented from markets for private short-term securities during this period of disintermediation. Because only bills were available in smaller denominations, households were able to shift deposit funds only into bills. Because corporations did not have sufficient bill holdings to arbitrage between the bill and private security markets, and commercial banks and municipalities had nonyield reasons for maintaining bill holdings, bill rates fell relative to other yields. As a result, expected inflation was not fully reflected in bill rates. In fact, the enormous disparity between private and U.S. short-term yields in 1974 was the driving force behind the creation of the money market fund, an entity that will prevent such disparities from recurring.

1.3   Inflation and Relative Returns on Equities, Bonds, and Bills

The first two columns in Table 1.2 repeat the same columns in Table 1.1 (except that 1979 and 1980 are excluded). The third and fourth columns record the mean and standard deviation of the difference between the

2. Preliminary data for 1981 suggest that the +2 percent peak in the 1952–80 period will be far exceeded. It appears that the real bill rate for 1981 will be greater than +5 percent.

Table 1.2   **Annual Inflation and the Returns on Equities (Relative to Bonds) and Bonds (Relative to Bills)**

	Inflation Rate		Corporate Equities Less Bonds		Treasury Bonds Less Bills	
	Mean	Std. Dev.	Mean	Std. Dev.	Mean	Std. Dev.
1926–40	−1.5	4.0	2.2	28.7	3.8	5.3
1941–51	6.0	5.3	13.2	14.8	1.5	4.0
1952–67	1.5	1.2	12.6	19.7	−1.1	5.8
1968–78	7.1	3.1	−0.5	13.1	−1.1	7.4
1926–51	1.7	5.9	6.9	24.4	2.8	5.0
1952–78	4.0	3.6	7.3	18.5	−1.1	6.5

SOURCES: The inflation rate is the rate of change in the consumer price index prior to 1947 and of the consumer price index net of shelter (to exclude the effect of changes in mortgage rates) after 1946. The other series are from Ibbotson and Sinquefield (1980).

annual returns earned on equities and corporate bonds. Equities earned a seven percentage point premium over both the 1926–51 and 1952-78 subperiods. However, when these periods are further subdivided, the enormous variability of this premium becomes apparent. The premium was much greater in the 1940s, 1950s, and 1960s than in the 1930s and 1970s.[3] It would appear from these data that there is no simple relationship between the premium and either the mean or the standard deviation of the inflation rate. Nonetheless, two of my coauthors in this volume have argued elsewhere that increased inflation combined with the excessive taxation of corporate income (Feldstein) and increased uncertainty regarding inflation and the economy generally (Malkiel) are causes of the relatively poor performance of equities during the past fifteen years. My own view is that these phenomena explain the relatively modest rise in promised new-issue debt yields (decline in real after-tax yields), but not the sharp decline in share values (Hendershott 1981).

The last two columns in Table 1.2 report the mean and standard deviation of the difference between the annual returns earned on U.S. government bonds and one-month bills. The difference was extraordinarily large, 3.8 percent, in the 1926–40 period, and it was a −1.1 percent in the 1952–67 and 1968–78 periods. These differences are due to apparently unanticipated movements in interest rates. To illustrate, if yields fall unexpectedly, then prices of long-term bonds will rise unexpectedly, and the one-year return on bonds will be large. This was apparently the case in the 1930s (the one-month bill rate declined from an average of over 3.0 percent in 1926–30 to less than 0.5 percent in the 1933–40 period). In contrast, if yields rise unexpectedly, then prices of

3. The premium that equities earned over Treasury bills is very similar except for the 1926–40 interval. As is indicated in the last column of Table 1.2, government bonds outperformed government bills by nearly four percentage points per annum in this period, with the result that the equity premium over bills was much larger than that over bonds.

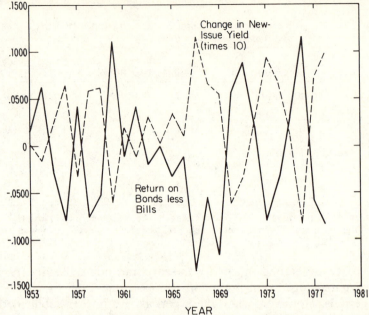

Fig. 1.2   Difference between Realized Annual Returns on Bonds and
Bills and the Change in the New-Issue Bond Rate, 1953–78.

long-term bonds will fall unexpectedly, and the one-year return on bonds
will be low. This apparently has happened in the post-1952 period (the
one-month bill rate rose from 1.5 percent in 1952–55 to 4 percent in
1964–67 to over 6 percent in 1973–78).

It is important to note that only unanticipated movements in interest
rates have such impacts on the difference in realized returns on bonds and
bills. For example, if long-term bond rates were expected to rise during
the year, then bonds would be priced at the beginning of the year such
that a high income return would offset the anticipated capital loss. In this
case, the difference in ex post returns on bonds and bills would be
independent of observed changes in new-issue bond yields. To determine
whether changes in bond yields have been anticipated or unanticipated,
yield data on new-issue equivalent twenty-year U.S. government bonds
were collected.[4] Figure 1.2 contains plots of the difference in ex post
annual yields on bonds and bills (the "maturity" premium of Ibbotson
and Sinquefield) for the 1953–78 period and the change in the new-issue
bond yield (scaled by a factor of 10) between the beginning and the end of
the same year. The striking negative correlation implies that the changes
in bond yields were unanticipated and have been the primary determinant of differences in the realized yields on bonds and bills.

4. The data were kindly supplied by Huston McCulloch. See note 1 for a reference
describing construction of the data.

Table 1.3   Business Cycle Reference Dates, 1926–80

Business Cycle Reference Dates		Duration in Months	
		Contraction (Trough from Previous Peak)	Expansion (Trough to Following Peak)
Trough	Peak		
Nov 1927	Aug 1929	13	21
Mar 1933	May 1937	43	50
June 1938	Feb 1945	13	80
Oct 1945	Nov 1948	8	37
Oct 1949	July 1953	11	45
May 1954	Aug 1957	10	39
Apr 1958	Apr 1960	8	24
Feb 1961	Dec 1969	10	106
Nov 1970	Nov 1973	11	36
Mar 1975	(Jan 1980)	16	58
Average, all cycles:			
10 cycles, 1926–78		14[a]	50[b]
5 cycles, 1926–53		18[a]	47[b]
5 cycles, 1953–78		11	53[b]

[a]11 months, excluding the Depression.
[b]39 months, excluding the World War II and Vietnam cycles.
SOURCE: National Bureau of Economic Research, Inc.

1.4   The Business Cycle and Returns on Equities and Bonds

Our next effort is to determine whether the performance of equity investments is particularly superior or inferior to that of bond investments during any stage of the business cycle. The National Bureau's reference dates, which are employed as a general guide to the stages of the business cycle, are listed in Table 1.3. In the 1926–78 period, ten full cycles occurred. Excluding the 43-month depression, contractions have ranged from 8 to 16 months and have had an average duration of 11 months. Excluding the 80 and 106 month wartime (World War II and Vietnam) expansions, upswings have varied from 21 to 58 months in duration and have averaged 39 months.

Annualized differences in equity and bond returns over different phases of the cycle have been compared. For contractions, the first and last five months (which overlap for the two eight-month contractions) were examined. For expansions, the first, second, third, and last six months were studied (the last two periods overlap during the twenty-one-month upswing in the late 1920s). The cycles were divided into the 1926–52 and 1953–78 subperiods, and means and standard deviations of the differences in equity and bond returns were calculated for the five pre-1953 cycles, the five post-1952 cycles, and all ten cycles. A quick examination of the data revealed that equities tend to earn a relatively superior return (recall that on average the annualized return on equities exceeds that on bonds by 7 percent) late in contractions and early in expansions and a relatively inferior return late in expansions and early in contractions.

Table 1.4 has been constructed to highlight these results. The means (and standard deviations) over all ten cycles in the 1926–78 period are listed at the bottom of the table. The mean net return on equities is 20 percent in the last five months of contractions (column 1) and 38 percent in the first six months of expansions (column 2). On the other hand, this net return is − 20 percent in the first five months of contractions (column 5). (The mean net return during the other six-month phases of the expansions was around the normal 6 percent.) While the mean net equity returns are large (in absolute value) during these periods, their variability is also large. Statistically, this is revealed by the fact that none of these means is twice the size of its standard error. Inspection of the individual cycle datum also indicates numerous "outliers."

The most pronounced outlier is the net equity return in the recovery of 1933, 125 percent; the other net returns in the first six months of upswings in the pre-1952 period vary within the narrow 23 to 36 percent band. Interestingly, the second-most-pronounced outlier appears to be the return in the immediately preceding period, the end of the 1932–33 contraction. Rather than the normally high return, − 37 percent was earned. Thus, the incredibly high return in the middle of 1933 is largely a catch-up for or offset to the low return in late 1932 and early 1933. The return over the full late-contraction–early-expansion period seems to be roughly in line with those around other lower turning points. Moreover, the same pattern occurs in 1957, when the highest post-1952 excess return early in the upswing, 50 percent, is preceded by the only negative excess return in the late-contraction months. It would appear that the variance in net equity returns over the full late-contraction–early-expansion period would be considerably less than the variance in returns in either the late-contraction or early-upswing months. The third column in Table 1.4 indicates that this is indeed the case. The mean net return on equities for the last six months of a contraction and first six months of the following expansion over all cycles is 26 percent, and it has a standard deviation of only 7 percent. Moreover, this is also roughly the case for both the first and last five cycles. Thus, the net equity returns are significantly positive at the 0.05 level, and this is true even if the "normal" net return of 6 percent is taken into account.

A somewhat similar pattern appears in late expansions and early contractions during the post-1953 period. The two largest negative net equity returns in early-recession months (column 5), − 46 percent in late

Table 1.4 Annualized Difference between Returns on Equities and Bonds over Various Stages of the Business Cycle (Percent)

	Returns around Troughs			Returns around Peaks		
	Last 5 Months of Contraction	First 6 Months of Expansion	Last 6 Months of Contraction and First 6 Months of Expansion	Last 6 Months of Expansion	First 5 Months of Contraction	Last 6 Months of Expansion and First 6 Months of Next Contraction
1926–52						
Apr 26–Feb 29	38	34	35	22	16	21
Feb 29–Nov 36	–37	125	16	53	–73	–9
Nov 36–Aug 44	22	25	25	–8	–58	–34
Aug 44–May 48	28	23	28	21	9	23
May 48–Jan 52	30	36	29	–19	0	–12
Mean	16	48	27	14	–21	–3
Std. Dev.	27	38	6	25	37	22
1953–78						
Jan 53–Feb 57	42	36	39	–5	–5	–1
Feb 57–Oct 59	–8	50	23	24	–46	–8
Oct 59–June 69	39	21	22	–17	–11	–13
June 69–May 73	21	25	17	6	–39	–16
May 73–Dec 78	24	5	23	–17	7	–9
Mean	24	27	25	–2	–18	–9
Std. Dev.	18	15	7	15	20	5
Total Period						
Mean	20	38	26	6	–20	–6
Std. Dev.	23	39	7	22	30	16

1957 and −39 percent in early 1970, were preceded by the only positive net equity returns in late expansions (column 4), 24 percent and 6 percent, respectively. The last column in Table 1.4 reports the net equity return over the last six months of an expansion and the first six months of the following recession; all are negative in the 1953–78 period. Moreover, the mean net extraordinary return (the −9 percent return less the normal 6 percent) for these five cycles is −15 percent with a 5 percent standard deviation. Thus, the net extraordinary returns are significantly negative in the late stages of the expansion and the early stages of the contraction. (This is not true, however, for cycles prior to 1953).

A possible problem with the above calculations is the comparison of the net returns around turning points with a constant "normal" 6 percent return. The mean net annual return on equities was shown in Table 1.2 to vary widely between different "eras"; the net return was only 2 percent in the 1926–40 period, about 13 percent in the 1941–67 span, and actually negative in the recent 1968–78 years. This suggests that net returns around turning points should be compared with the average net returns in surrounding years, rather than over the entire half-century. To accomplish this, we have first divided the months between January 1926 and December 1978 into three types of periods: those around troughs in which equity returns appear to be superior; those around peaks in which equity returns appear to be relatively inferior; and the remainder. The inferior periods are defined as the last six months of every expansion and the first half (dropping fractions) or first six months, whichever is less, of every contraction. The superior periods are defined as the last half (dropping fractions) or last six months, whichever is less, of every contraction and the first six months of every expansion. The second step in this comparison is to divide the total 1926–78 period into ten overlapping intervals that contain single adjoining peaks and troughs and all the surrounding months that do not overlap with adjacent superior and inferior periods. That is, the intervals extend from six months after a trough to six months before the second following peak. These ten overlapping intervals are listed at the left in Table 1.5. Also listed are the arithmetic means (annualized) during the superior periods within the interval, the inferior periods, and all months excluding such periods. The mean in the latter months is the "normal" return with which the mean returns around the trough and peak are compared.

The comparison is made in columns 4 and 5, where the normal return has been subtracted from the superior and inferior returns, respectively. These results are even more striking than those in Table 1.4. The extraordinary net returns on equities around troughs average 24 percent, and no net return is less than 14 percent. In contrast, the extraordinary net returns on equities are negative around all peaks except that at the end of World War II. The average net return around peaks is −15 percent. If

Table 1.5   **Annualized Difference between Returns on Equities and Bonds Near Troughs, Near Peaks, and in Other Periods (Percent)**

	Near Troughs	Near Peaks	Other Months	Excess Near Troughs	Excess Near Peaks
Jan 26–Feb 29	35	20	21	14	−1
June 28–Nov 36	30	−4	1	29	−5
Oct 33–Aug 44	34	−32	8	26	−40
Jan 39–May 48	31	21	4	27	17
May 46–Jan 53	36	−9	13	23	−22
May 50–Feb 57	43	−5	21	22	−26
Dec 54–Oct 59	45	−11	18	27	−29
Nov 58–June 69	31	−12	8	23	−20
Sept 61–May 73	23	−13	5	18	−18
June 71–Dec 78	23	−9	−4	27	−5
Mean	33	−5	10	24	−15
Std. Dev.	7	16	9	5	17

the analysis is restricted to the last six cycles, then the average extraordinary net return on equities around peaks is −20 percent and the standard deviation is only 6 percent.

1.5 Summary

The results of our investigation of the impacts over the past half-century of inflation and the business cycle on realized yields on equities, long-term debt, and short-term debt can be summarized in terms of three relationships. Each is presented in turn.

First, prior to the Treasury–Federal Reserve Accord in 1951, nominal yields on one-month Treasury bills were reasonably stable while real bill rates were incredibly volatile. This was largely due to the nonnegativity constraint on nominal bill rates during the rapid deflation in the early 1930s (and 1938 and 1949, to a lesser extent) and the pegging (at low levels) of nominal interest rates during the rapid inflation early in World War II and in the Korean conflict and following the former. Since 1952, the reverse has been true. Nominal bill rates have cycled around a rising trend, and real bill rates have stayed near zero. Short-term bills have been a hedge against inflation during the past thirty years.

Second, changes in long-term new-issue bond yields have been largely unanticipated, and these changes have dominated the realized returns on bonds relative to Treasury bills. Because bond rates have risen with (unexpected) inflation during the past fifteen years, bonds have earned negative real returns.

Third, the relative returns on equities and bonds are greatly affected by the business cycle with equities performing very well around troughs and very poorly around peaks. Extraordinary net (of bond returns) equity returns have averaged 24 percent per annum in the (roughly) year surrounding troughs over the ten cycles since 1926 and have never been less than 14 percent. In contrast, these returns have averaged −20 percent in the (roughly) year surrounding peaks over the six cycles since 1946 and have never been higher than −5 percent.

References

Cook, Timothy Q. 1981. The Determinants of Spreads between Treasury Bill and Other Market Rates. *Journal of Economics and Business* 33: 177–187.

Hendershott, Patric H. 1981. The Decline in Aggregate Share Values: Taxation, Valuation Errors, Risk and Profitability. *American Economic Review* 71:

Hendershott, Patric H., and Huang, Roger D. 1983. Debt and Equity Yields. In Friedman, Benjamin, ed., *Financial Capital Structure in the American Economy*, Chicago: University of Chicago Press.

Ibbotson, Roger G., and Sinquefield, Rex A. 1979. Stocks, Bonds, Bills and Inflation: Updates. *Financial Analysts Journal*, pp. 40–44.

Ibbotson, Roger G., and Sinquefield, Rex A. 1980. *Stocks, Bonds, Bills and Inflation; Historical Returns (1926–1978)*. Financial Analysts Research Foundation, University of Virginia, Charlottesville.

McCulloch, J. Huston. 1975. The Tax-Adjusted Yield Curve. *Journal of Finance* 30: 811–30.

2   Risk and Return: A New Look

Burton G. Malkiel

One of the best-documented propositions in the field of finance is that, on average, investors have received higher rates of return on investment securities for bearing greater risk. This chapter looks at the historical evidence regarding risk and return, explains the fundamentals of portfolio and asset-pricing theory, and then goes on to take a new look at the relationship between risk and return using some unexplored risk measures that seem to capture quite closely the actual risks being valued in the market.

2.1 Some Historical Evidence

Risk is a most slippery and elusive concept. It is hard for investors—let alone economists—to agree on a precise definition. The dictionary defines risk as the possibility of suffering harm or loss. If I buy one-year Treasury bills to yield, say, 10 percent and hold them until they mature, I am virtually certain of earning a 10 percent monetary return before income taxes. The possibility of loss is so small as to be considered nonexistent. But if I hold common stock in my local power and light company for one year on the basis of an anticipated 12.5 percent dividend return, the possibility of loss increases. The dividend of the company might be cut and, more important, the market price at the end of the year

Burton G. Malkiel is Professor of Economics and William S. Beinecke Professor of Management Studies at Yale University, and Dean of the Yale School of Organization and Management.

The research reported in this chapter has been supported by the National Bureau of Economic Research, the Institute for Quantitative Research in Finance, the John Weinberg Foundation, and the Princeton Financial Research Center. As indicated in note 3, the empirical tests reported at the end of the chapter are taken from a joint study with John G. Cragg of NBER and the University of British Columbia.

could be much lower, so that I might suffer a serious net loss. Risk is the chance that expected security returns will not materialize and, in particular, that the securities I hold will fall in price.

Once academics had accepted the idea that risk for investors is related to the chance of disappointment in achieving expected security returns, a natural measure suggested itself—the probable variability or dispersion of future returns. Thus, financial risk has generally been defined as the variance or standard deviation of returns.[1]

Empirical studies of broad classes of securities confirm the general relationship between risk and return. The most thorough recent study has been done by Ibbotson and Sinquefield (1979). Their data covered the period 1926 through 1978. The results are shown in Table 2.1.

A quick glance shows that, over long periods of time, common stocks have, on average, provided relatively generous total rates of return. These returns, including dividends and capital gains, have exceeded by a substantial margin the returns from long-term corporate bonds and U.S. Treasury bills. The stock returns have also tended to be well in excess of the inflation rate as measured by the annual rate of increase in consumer prices. The data show, however, that common stock returns are highly variable as measured by the standard deviation and the range of annual returns shown in the last three columns of the table. Returns from equities have ranged from a gain of over 50 percent (in 1933) to a loss of almost the same magnitude (in 1931). Clearly, the extra returns that have been available to investors from stocks have come at the expense of assuming considerably higher risk.

The patterns evident in Ibbotson and Sinquefield's chart also appear when the returns and risks of individual stock portfolios are compared. Indeed, most of the differences that exist in the returns from different mutual funds can be explained by differences in the risk they have assumed. However, there are ways in which investors can reduce the risks they take. This brings us to the subject of modern portfolio theory.

2.2 Reducing Risk: Modern Portfolio Theory

Portfolio theory begins with the premise that all investors are risk averse. They want high returns and guaranteed outcomes. The theory tells investors how to combine stocks in their portfolios to give them the least risk possible, consistent with the return they seek. It also gives a rigorous mathematical justification for the time-honored investment

1. Variance is defined as the average squared deviation of the (periodic) investment returns from their average. The square root of the variance is the standard deviation and is also often used to measure variability and, thus, risk. While it is true that only downward surprises constitute risk, as long as the distribution of returns is symmetric, a variance measure will serve as a good proxy for the chance of disappointment.

Table 2.1   Selected Performance Statistics, 1926–78

	Annual (Geometric) Mean Rate of Return	Number of Years Returns Are Positive	Number of Years Returns Are Negative	Highest Annual Return (and Year)	Lowest Annual Return (and Year)	Standard Deviation of Annual Returns
Common Stocks	8.9	35	18	54.0% (1933)	−43.3 (1931)	22.4
Long-term corporate bonds	4.0	43	10	18.4 (1970)	−8.1 (1969)	5.8
U.S. Treasury bills	2.5	52	1	8.0 (1974)	−0.0 (1940)	2.1
Consumer Price Index	2.5	43	10	18.2 (1946)	−10.3 (1932)	4.7

SOURCE: Ibbotson and Sinquefield (1979).

maxim that diversification is a sensible strategy for individuals who like to reduce their risks. The basic idea was that a portfolio of risky (volatile) stocks can be put together in such a way as to be less risky than any one of the individual stocks in it. A simple illustration will make the whole game clear.

Let us suppose we have an island economy with only two businesses. The first is a large resort with beaches, tennis courts, a golf course, and the like. The second is a manufacturer of umbrellas. Weather affects the fortunes of both. During sunny seasons the resort does a booming business and umbrella sales plummet. During rainy seasons the resort owner does very poorly, while the umbrella manufacturer enjoys high sales and large profits. Table 2.2 shows some hypothetical earnings for the two businesses during the different seasons. I assume that all earnings are paid out as dividends, so these are also the returns paid out to investors.

Suppose that, on average, one-half the seasons are sunny and one-half are rainy (i.e., the probability of a sunny or rainy season is one-half). An investor who bought stock in the umbrella manufacturer would find that half the time he earned a 50 percent return and half the time he lost 25 percent of his investment. On average, he would earn a return of 12.5 percent. This is what we call the investor's *expected return*. Similarly, investment in the resort would produce the same results. Investing in either one of these businesses would be fairly risky, however, because the results are quite variable, and there could be several sunny or rainy seasons in a row.

Suppose, however, that instead of buying only one security an investor with two dollars diversified and put half his money in the umbrella manufacturer's and half in the resort owner's business. In sunny seasons, a one-dollar investment in the resort would produce a fifty-cent return, while a one-dollar investment in the umbrella manufacturer would lose twenty-five cents. The investor's total return would be twenty-five cents, which is 12.5 percent of his total investment of two dollars.

Note that during rainy seasons exactly the same thing happens—only the names are changed. Investment in the umbrella manufacturer produces a good 50 percent return while the investment in the resort loses 25 percent. Again, however, the diversized investor makes a 12.5 percent return on his total investment.

This simple illustration points out the basic advantage of diversification. Whatever happens to the weather, and thus to the island economy, by diversifying investments over both of the firms an investor is sure of

Table 2.2   **An Example of Diversification**

	Umbrella Manufacturer	Resort Owner
Rainy season	50%	−25%
Sunny season	−25%	50%

making a 12.5 percent return each year. The trick that made the game work was that while both companies were risky (returns were variable from year to year), the companies were affected differently by weather conditions. As long as there is some lack of parallelism in the fortunes of the individual companies in the economy, diversification will always reduce risk. In the present case, where there is a perfect negative relationship between the companies' fortunes (one always does well when the other does poorly), diversification can totally eliminate risk.

Of course, there is always a rub, and the rub in this case is that the fortunes of most companies move pretty much in tandem. When there is a recession and people are unemployed, they may buy neither summer vacations nor umbrellas. Therefore, one should not expect in practice to get the neat total risk elimination just shown. Nevertheless, since company fortunes do not always move completely in parallel, investment in a diversified portfolio of stocks is likely to be less risky than investment in one or two single securities. While a portfolio of General Motors and its major steel and tire supplier would not reduce risk much, if at all, a portfolio of GM and a defense contractor in a depressed area might reduce risk substantially.

The example may seem a bit strained, and most investors will realize that when the market gets clobbered just about all stocks go down. Still, at least at certain times, some stocks do move against the market. Gold stocks are often given as an example of securities that do not typically move in the same direction as the general market. Similarly, international diversification can reduce risk. The point to realize in setting up a portfolio is that true diversification of a portfolio depends on having stocks that are not all dependent on the same economic variables (total spending in the economy, inflation rates, etc.). Wise investors will diversify their portfolios not by names or industries but by the determinants that influence the fluctuations of various securities.

2.3 Modeling Risk: The Capital-Asset Pricing Model (CAPM)

Portfolio theory has important implications for how stocks are actually valued. If investors seek to reduce risk in anything like the manner described by portfolio theorists, the stock market will tend to reflect these risk-reducing activities. This brings us to what is called the "Capital-Asset Pricing Model."

I have mentioned that the reason diversification cannot usually produce the miracle of risk elimination is that usually stocks tend to move up and down together. Still, diversification is worthwhile—it can eliminate some risks. What the CAPM did was to focus directly on what part of a security's risk could be eliminated by diversification and what part could not.

The theory begins by classifying the sources of the variability of an individual stock. Part of total risk or variability may be called the security's *systematic risk*, arising from the basic variability of stock prices in general and the tendency for all stocks to go along with the general market, at least to some extent. The remaining variability in a stock's returns is called *unsystematic risk* and results from factors peculiar to that particular company, for example, a strike, the discovery of a new product, and so on.

Systematic risk, also called market risk, captures the reaction of individual stocks (or portfolios) to general market swings. Some stocks and portfolios tend to be very sensitive to market movements. Others are more stable. This relative volatility or sensitivity to market moves can be estimated on the basis of the past record, and is popularly known as the beta calculation. This calculation is essentially a comparison between the movements of an individual stock (or portfolio) and the movements of the market as a whole. It is a numerical description of systematic risk.

The calculation begins by assigning a beta of 1 to a broad market index, such as the NYSE index or the S&P 500. If a stock has a beta of 2, then on average it swings twice as far as the market. If the market goes up 10 percent, the stock rises 20 percent. If a stock has a beta of 0.5, it tends to be more stable than the market (it will go up or down 5 percent when the market rises or declines 10 percent). Professionals often call high-beta stocks aggressive investments and label low-beta stocks as defensive.

Now the important thing to realize is that *systematic risk cannot be eliminated by diversification*. It is precisely because all stocks move more or less in tandem (a large share of their variability is systematic) that even diversified stock portfolios are risky. Indeed, if I diversified extremely broadly by buying a share in the S&P index (which by definition has a beta of 1), I would still have quite variable (risky) returns because the market as a whole fluctuates widely.

Unsystematic risk is the variability in stock prices (and, therefore, in returns from stocks) that results from factors peculiar to an individual company. Receipt of a large new contract, discovery of mineral resources on the company's property, labor difficulties, the revelation that the corporation's treasurer has had his hand in the company till—all can make a stock's price move independently of the market. The risk associated with such variability is precisely the kind that diversification can reduce. The whole point of portfolio theory was that, to the extent that stocks do not move in tandem all the time, variations in the returns from any one security will tend to be washed away or smoothed out by complementary variation in the returns from other securities.

Figure 2.1 illustrates the important relationship between diversification and total risk. Suppose we randomly selected securities for our portfolio that tended on average to be just as volatile as the market. (The average betas for the securities in our portfolio will always be equal to 1.)

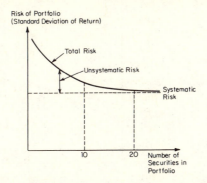

Fig. 2.1   How Diversification Reduces Risk. From Franco Modigliani and Gerald A. Pogue, "An Introduction to Risk and Return," *The Financial Analyst Journal*, March–April 1974.

Figure 2.1 shows that as we add more securities, the total risk of our portfolio declines, especially at the start.

When ten securities are selected for our portfolio, a good deal of the unsystematic risk is eliminated, and additional diversification yields little further risk reduction. By the time twenty securities are in the portfolio, the unsystematic part of risk is substantially eliminated, and our portfolio (with a beta of 1) will tend to move up and down essentially in tandem with the market.

Now comes the key step in the argument. Both financial theorists and practitioners had agreed for years that investors should be compensated for taking on more risk by receiving a higher expected return. Stock prices must therefore adjust to offer higher returns where more risk is perceived, to ensure that all securities are held by someone. What is different about the new theory is the definition and measurement of risk. Before the advent of the CAPM, it was often suggested that the return on each security would be related to the total risk inherent in that security. It was believed that the return from holding a security would vary with the instability of that security's particular performance, that is, with the variability or standard deviation of the returns it produced. The new theory says that the *total* risk of each individual security is irrelevant. Only the systematic component of that total instability is relevant for valuation. Because stocks can be combined in portfolios to eliminate specific risk (see Figure 2.1), only the undiversifiable or systematic part of the risk will command a risk premium (i.e., an extra return over and above that obtainable from a riskless asset). Investors will not get paid for bearing risks that can be diversified away. The only part of total risk that investors will get paid for bearing is systematic risk, the risk that diversification cannot eliminate. This is the basic logic behind the CAPM.

If investors did get an extra return (a risk premium) for bearing unsystematic risk, diversified portfolios made up of stocks with large

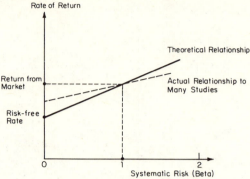

Rate of Return

Theoretical Relationship

Return from Market

Actual Relationship to Many Studies

Risk-free Rate

0   1   2

Systematic Risk (Beta)

Fig. 2.2   Risk and Return According to the Capital-Asset Pricing Model. Rate of return = risk-free rate + beta × (return from market − risk-free rate). In other words, the return you get on any stock or portfolio increases directly with the beta value you assume. From *A Random Walk down Wall Street*, 2d college ed. © 1981 by Burton G. Malkiel. Used with permission of the publishers, W. W. Norton & Company, Inc.

amounts of unsystematic risk would give larger returns than equally risky portfolios of stocks with less unsystematic risk. Investors would snap at these higher returns by bidding up the prices of stocks with large unsystematic risk and selling stocks with equivalent betas but lower unsystematic risk. This would continue until the prospective returns of stocks with the same betas were equalized and no risk premium could be obtained for bearing unsystematic risk. Thus, the CAPM says that returns for any stock (or portfolio) will be related to beta, the systematic risk that cannot be diversified away. Any other results would be inconsistent with the existence of efficient markets.

The key relationship of the theory is shown in Figure 2.2 (For the moment, ignore the dashed line in the diagram.) As the systematic risk (beta) of an individual stock (or portfolio) increases, so does the return an investor should expect. If an investor's portfolio has a beta of zero, as might be the case if all his funds were invested in a very short-term Treasury bill (beta would be zero since the returns from the certificate would not vary at all with swings in the stock market), the investor would receive some modest rate of return, which is generally called the risk-free rate of interest.[2] As the individual takes on more risk, however, the return should increase. If the investor holds a portfolio with a beta of 1 (for example, one share in one of the broad stock market averages), his return will equal the general return from common stocks. This return has over long periods of time exceeded the risk-free rate of interest, but the investment is a risky one. In certain periods the return is much less than

2. Of course, the yield from a Treasury bill is risk free only in a nominal sense. An investor will be guaranteed a certain money rate of return from the investment but his/her real rate of return will be uncertain. The risk-return relationships described here concern relationships between nominal returns before inflation and before taxes.

the risk-free rate and involves taking substantial losses. This, as we have said, is precisely what is meant by risk.

Figure 2.2 shows that a number of different expected returns are possible simply by adjusting the beta of the portfolio. For example, suppose an investor put half of her money in a T-bill and half in a share of the market averages. In this case she would receive a return midway between the risk-free return and the return from the market, and her portfolio would have an average beta of 0.5. The theory then asserts very simply that to get a higher average long-run rate of return, one must simply increase the beta of the portfolio. An investor can get a portfolio with a beta larger than 1 either by buying high-beta stocks or by purchasing a portfolio with average volatility on margin.

2.4   Tests of the CAPM Model

Tests of the CAPM have tried to ascertain if security returns are in fact directly related to beta, as the theory asserts. The early evidence seemed to support the theory. The relationship between the performance of a large number of professionally managed funds and the beta measure of relative volatility was generally consistent with the theory. The portfolio returns have varied positively with beta in roughly a straight-line manner, as is shown in Figure 2.3, so that over the long pull, high-beta portfolios have provided larger total returns than low-risk ones.

Unfortunately, however, as more evidence accumulated, a number of disquieting results came to light. First, the measured actual risk-return

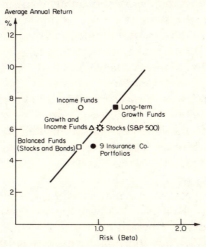

Fig. 2.3   Average Annual Return versus Risk: Selected Institutional Investors, 1965–78. Source: Buck Consultants, Inc. From *The Inflation Beater's Investment Guide: Winning Strategies for the 1980s.* © 1980 by Burton G. Malkiel. Used with permission of the publishers, W. W. Norton & Company, Inc.

relationships found in the market appear to be much flatter than those implied by the theory. In Figure 2.2, for example, the actual measured relationships have usually looked more like the dashed line than the solid line, which represents the theoretical relationship. There seems to be a phenomenon much like that found at the racetrack, in that low-risk stocks earn higher returns and high-risk stocks earn lower returns than the theory predicts. (At the racetrack, long shots seem to go off at much lower odds than their true probability of winning would indicate, whereas favorites go off at higher odds than is consistent with their winning percentages.)

The divergence of theory from evidence is even more striking in the short run. For some short periods, it may happen that risk and return are *negatively* related. In 1972, for example, which was an up-market year, it turned out that safer (lower-beta) stocks went up more than did *more* volatile securities. *Fortune* magazine commented dryly on this well-publicized failure: "The results defied the textbooks." What happened was that in 1972, styles changed in Wall Street, as institutional investors eschewed younger, more speculative companies, the "faded ladies" of the late 1960s, and became much more enamored of the highest quality, most stable leading corporations in the so-called first tier of stocks. It became clear that beta could not be used to guarantee investors a predictable performance over periods of a few months or even a year. And even over some longer periods of time—when the market has produced a positive rate of return—investors have actually been penalized for taking on more risk.

Another problem the theory encounters is the instability of measured betas. The beta of a stock is measured on the basis of historical relationships between returns for that stock and the returns from the market. It turns out that these past betas for individual stocks are relatively poor predictors of future betas. While the problem is less severe for portfolios, which are averages of many stocks, it is clear that past betas are quite imperfect estimates of future volatility numbers. Moreover, as Roll (1977) has pointed out, it is impossible to observe the market's return against which we measure beta. In principle, the market includes *all* stocks, a variety of other financial instruments, and even nonmarketable assets. The Standard and Poor's Index (or any other index) is a very imperfect market proxy at best. And, when we measure "market risk" using imperfect proxies, we may obtain quite imperfect estimates of market sensitivity. Roll (1977) showed that by changing the market index against which betas are measured, one can obtain quite different measures of the risk level of individual stocks or portfolios and thus quite different predictions of future returns. It is clear, then, that in judging risk, beta cannot be a substitute for brains.

2.5 Toward a Broader Method of Risk Measurement

To understand the logic of the risk measurement system proposed here, it is important to remember the correct insight underlying the CAPM. The only risk that investors should be compensated for bearing is the risk that cannot be diversified away. Only systematic risk will command a risk premium in the market. But, the systematic elements of risk in particular stocks and portfolios may be far more complicated than can be captured by a beta measure—the tendency of stocks to move more or less than any particular stock index.

Let us take a look at several other potential systematic risk elements. Changes in National Income, for example, may affect returns from individual stocks in a systematic way. This was mentioned earlier in the illustration of a simple island economy. During a recession, consumers might buy neither vacations nor umbrellas. Changes in National Income also mirror the changes in the personal income available to individuals, and so the systematic relationship between security returns and salary income can be expected to be important elements in individual behavior. For example, the worker in a Ford plant will find that a holding of Ford common stock is particularly risky since job layoffs and poor returns from Ford stock are likely to occur at the same time. Changes in National Income may also reflect changes in other forms of property income and may therefore be relevant for institutional portfolio managers as well.

Changes in interest rates also systematically affect the returns from individual stocks and are important nondiversifiable risk elements. To the extent that stocks tend to suffer as interest rates go up, equities are a risky investment, and those stocks that are particularly vulnerable to increases in the general level of interest rates are especially risky. Since fixed-income securities are included in the portfolios of many institutional investors, this systematic risk factor is particularly important for some of the largest investors in the market. Clearly, then, investors who think of risk in its broadest and most meaningful sense will be sensitive to the tendency of stocks to be affected by changes in interest rates.

Changes in the rate of inflation will similarly tend to have systematic influences on the returns from common stocks. This is so for at least two reasons. First, an increase in the rate of inflation tends to increase interest rates and thus may lead to the lower prices of equities just discussed. Second, increases in inflation may squeeze profit margins for certain groups of companies such as public utilities, which often find that rate increases lag behind increases in their costs. On the other hand, inflation may benefit the prices of some common stocks, such as those in natural resource industries. Thus, again there are important systematic relationships between stock returns and economic variables that may not be captured adequately by a simple beta measure of risk.

The final new risk variable introduced is a measure of the dispersion among Wall Street security analysts concerning the future earnings and dividend growth of the company. If analysts differ greatly in their growth forecasts for a company, we shall consider the stock to be relatively risky. At first glance, this forecast dispersion variable may seem like a measure of total variability for a company—precisely the kind of measure that was used before the advent of the Capital-Asset Pricing Model. While such an interpretation is possible, the dispersion of analysts' forecasts may actually serve as a particularly useful proxy for a variety of systematic risks. The following illustration will explain why.

Suppose we had two companies, one a steel company that is extremely sensitive to systematic influences in the economy, the other a pharmaceutical firm that is quite insensitive to economic conditions. It may be that Wall Street analysts agree completely on how economic conditions will affect the two companies, but still differ greatly on their economic forecasts. If this were so, there could be a big dispersion in earnings forecasts for the steel company (because of the differences in economic forecasts and the sensitivity of the company to economic conditions), and very small differences in forecasts in the drug company (because economic conditions have little effect on that company).

Table 2.3 illustrates the situation. Analyst 1 is optimistic about real growth and convinced that inflation and interest rates will fall. Analyst 2 predicts sluggish real growth but believes that inflation and interest rates will remain high. The analysts may agree completely on how economic conditions affect the two companies. Nevertheless, they can differ in their earnings forecasts, because their economic forecasts differ and the two companies are not equally sensitive to these economic conditions. The steel company is very sensitive to GNP growth because it affects sales, to inflation because it affects raw material prices, and to interest rates because they affect borrowing costs. Thus, analyst 1 sees strong earnings growth for the steel company while analyst 2 predicts a very weak performance. As for the drug company, since, by assumption, it is relatively unaffected by economic conditions, the analysts agree on their earnings forecasts despite differences in their economic forecasts. The important point to note about this illustration is that the company for which the forecasts differed was the company most sensitive to systematic risk factors, i.e., the company with the greatest systematic sensitivity to economic conditions. Hence, differences in analysts' forecasts may be a most useful proxy for systematic risk in the broadest sense of the term.

2.6   Some Statistical Tests

It is possible to test statistically the influence of variable risk factors on anticipated rates of return for different common stocks. We hypothesize

Table 2.3   **How Economic Forecasts Affect Earnings Forecasts**

	Economic Forecast	Steel Company Forecast	Drug Company Forecast
Analyst 1	GNP: up sharply Inflation: down Interest rates: down	Sales up Raw material prices steady Borrowing costs down	Sales up whatever happens to GNP Uses few raw materials—no effect No borrowing—no effect
		Strong earnings growth	Strong earnings growth
Analyst 2	GNP: no growth Inflation: remains high Interest rates: remain high	Sales flat Raw material prices up Borrowing costs up	Sales up whatever happens to GNP Uses few raw materials—no effect No borrowing—no effect
		Weak earnings growth	Strong earnings growth

that stocks with larger systematic risks ought to promise investors a higher expected rate of return—the bigger the risk, the larger should be the reward.[3] Several alternative measures of systematic risk were used in the analysis.

1. Market Risk: Market risk is measured by beta, the historical sensitivity of the stock to swings in the overall market index. Stocks very sensitive to fluctuations in the overall market are riskier and therefore should provide higher anticipated rates of return.

2. Economic Activity Risk: This risk measures the sensitivity of an individual stock to movements in the level of National Income. It is estimated on the basis of past sensitivity of a security's return to changes in National Income. Stocks that are more sensitive to fluctuations in economic activity will have more systematic risk and hence ought to offer a larger rate of return.

3. Inflation Risk: Stocks which tend systematically to produce very poor returns when inflation accelerates are considered to have large systematic risk with respect to inflation. Hence, stocks with greater inflation risk should offer a higher anticipated rate of return.

4. Interest Rate Risk: Stocks which are extremely sensitive to interest rates also contain greater systematic risk. Alternatively, stocks that do well when interest rates rise would be particularly valuable in portfolios which contain both stocks and bonds. Thus, stocks that are particularly sensitive to change in market interest rates should be considered riskier and hence command a larger prospective rate of return.

5. Dispersion of Analysts' Forecasts: As indicated above, this risk variable may serve as a good proxy for a variety of systematic risk. The larger the dispersion of forecasts, the larger the anticipated return ought to be to the holder of securities.

The hypothesis to be tested is that expected returns on individual stocks should be related to a variety of risk variables. In order to perform the test, however, we need some way of measuring expected returns on individual stocks. We also need expectational data on the forecasts of security analysts from which we can measure the forecast dispersion mentioned above. Fortunately, a long-standing study done at Princeton's Financial Research Center has provided the expectational data we need. For each year during the 1960s, data were collected from a number of leading investment houses on forecasts of the long-run growth of dividends and earnings for a substantial sample of investment-grade issues. We also obtained similar data for the end of 1980 from the Institutional Brokerage Estimate System (IBES) of the investment firm of Lynch, Jones, and Ryan. The IBES provided estimates of long-run earnings growth as well as the dispersion of forecasts.

---

3. A formal theoretical justification for the hypothesis tested can be found in Malkiel and Cragg (1980). See also Ross (1976).

Anticipated rates of return on individual common stocks were derived from the standard dividend discount valuation model. According to that model the worth of a common stock is equal to the present value of the future stream of dividends an investor can expect to receive from that stock. It turns out that this model has a very simple implication. The expected rate of return on any stock can be derived by summing the dividend yield of the stock and the long-run expected growth rate of the earnings and dividends per share. An example will make the calculations clear. Say that American Telephone and Telegraph is selling at a dividend yield of approximately 10.5 percent. Say the average Wall Street forecast for the long-run expected growth rate of dividends is 6 percent. It will then turn out that a long-run holder of AT&T common stock can expect a 16.5 percent rate of return from holding AT&T stock. This is made up of a 10.5 percent dividend yield plus a 6 percent growth rate.[4]

We have now discussed the measurement of all the variables used in the study as well as the hypothesis to be tested. We turn next to the results of the analysis. Table 2.4 shows the statistical relationship between expected rates of return for a sample of individual stocks and the five risk measures listed above. While the pairwise correlation coefficients are not terribly high they are statistically significant in most instances. Thus, the results indicate that each of these risk variables does seem to be important in explaining the structure of anticipated returns. The t-statistics also support this conclusion. A handy rough rule is that any t-statistic larger than 2 indicates a statistically significant relationship.

While the traditional beta measure of risk does seem to be related to expected returns in the manner described by the theory, it appears that there are a variety of systematic risk influences on individual stocks and portfolios. Systematic susceptibility to economic conditions as measured by National Income, interest rates, and the rate of inflation also seems to play an important role in explaining differences in expected returns. This can be seen by looking at the correlation coefficients relating each risk measure to expected returns and by examining the t-values. The fact that so many of the t-values are statistically significant in the table suggests that several systematic risk influences clearly influence expected returns. Moreover, when several of these systematic risk influences are used together, a far better explanation of differences in expected returns is

---

4. If we assume that the price-earnings multiple and dividend yield do not change, even a short-run holder can expect the same 16.5 percent rate of return. This is so because by assumption the stock's value will grow at 6.0 percent because of the increase in dividends and earnings. Hence, an individual selling AT&T stock after a year would realize 6.0 percent appreciation as well as a 10.5 percent dividend return. Although the results are not reported here, anticipated rates of return were also derived from a somewhat different version of the standard valuation model that allowed for variable long-term growth rates. The results were quite similar to those obtained from the simple model, and only the results from the standard model are reported here.

Table 2.4   Association of Risk Measures and Expected Returns (Correlation Coefficients and T-Values of Regression Coefficients)

	Market Risk (Beta)		Economy Risk		Inflation Risk		Interest Rate Risk		Dispersion of Analysis Forecasts	
	Corr. Coef.	T-Value	Corr. Coef.	T-Value	Corr. Coef.	T-Value	Corr. Coef.	T-Value	Corr. Coef.	T-Value
1961	.32	3.65	.32	3.98	.11	1.31	.03	0.36	.25	2.57
1962	.26	3.32	.29	3.84	.08	1.03	.07	0.93	.44	6.30
1963	.04	0.55	.21	2.70	.10	1.29	.10	1.22	.28	3.74
1964	.13	1.65	.22	2.87	.18	2.24	.22	2.89	.42	5.95
1965	.29	3.79	.26	3.42	.24	3.17	.25	3.31	.47	6.97
1966	.39	5.35	.25	3.27	.40	5.40	.37	4.90	.22	2.79
1967	.31	3.49	.30	3.85	.47	6.59	.43	5.74	.20	2.54
1968	.27	3.35	.32	3.91	.49	6.50	.39	4.97	.74	12.86
1980	.27	4.56	.21	3.24	.16	2.56	.05	0.78	.31	5.29

Table 2.5		Multiple Correlation Coefficients Using All Five Risk Variables Together

Year	Multiple Correlation Coefficient
1961	.44
1962	.49
1963	.37
1964	.52
1965	.48
1966	.45
1967	.54
1968	.80
1980	.38

found than can be obtained using any single measure alone. This can be seen by comparing the multiple correlation coefficients in Table 2.5 with the single-variable correlations shown in Table 2.4.[5] Although this is not shown in the table, it should be noted that several of the risk variables were statistically significant in each year. This indicates that several systematic risk elements influence expected security returns.

If, however, we wanted for simplicity to select the one risk measure that is most closely related to expected returns, the traditional beta measure would probably not be our first choice. The best single risk proxy appears to be the dispersion of analysts' forecasts. This risk measure generally produced the highest correlations with expected returns and the highest t-values in Table 2.4. Companies for which there is a broad consensus with respect to future earnings and dividends seem to be less risky (and hence have lower expected returns) than companies for which there is little agreement among security analysts. It is possible to interpret this result as contradicting modern asset-pricing theory, which suggests that total variability per se will not be relevant for valuation. As we have shown, however, this dispersion of forecasts could well result if different companies were particularly susceptible to systematic risk elements, and thus our dispersion measure may be the best individual proxy available to capture the variety of systematic risk elements to which securities are subject.

2.7 Implications of the Analysis

The quest for better risk measures is not simply an amusing exercise that accomplishes only the satisfaction of permitting academics to play

5. In general, the correlations are not as close for 1980. 1980 used a different data set and is therefore not directly comparable. The general findings for 1980 are similar, however.

with their computers. It has important implications for protecting investors. A good illustration of how a better understanding of the many facets of risk can aid investors is provided by the recent fascination with so-called yield-tilted index funds, which had gained a considerable following in the investment community by the 1980s. Yield-tilted index funds tried to match closely the general composition of one of the broad stock indices such as the S&P 500 stock index, but their portfolios were tilted toward relatively high yield stocks. Such funds were being especially recommended for tax-exempt investors.

The reasoning behind the yield-tilted index fund seemed appealingly plausible. Since dividends are generally taxed more highly than capital gains, and since the market equilibrium is presumably achieved on the basis of after-tax returns, the equilibrium pretax returns for stocks that pay high dividends ought to be higher than for securities which produce lower dividends and correspondingly higher capital gains. Hence, the tax-exempt investor should specialize in buying high-dividend-paying stocks. In order to avoid the assumption of any greater risk than is involved in buying the market index, however, this tax-exempt investor was advised to purchase a yield-tilted *index* fund, that is, a very broadly diversified portfolio of high-dividend paying stocks that mirrored the market index in the sense that it had a beta coefficient precisely equal to one.

Even on a priori grounds one might question the logic of the yield-tilted index fund. Many of the largest investors in the market are tax-exempt (such as pension and endowment funds), and other investors (such as corporations) actually pay a higher tax on capital gains than on dividend income.[6] Thus, it is far from clear that many of the most important investors in the stock market prefer to receive income through capital gains rather than through dividend payments. But apart from these a priori arguments, the statistical results just reviewed can be interpreted as providing another argument against the yield-tilted index fund.

If the traditional beta calculation does not provide a full description of systematic risk, the yield-tilted index fund may well fail to mirror the market index. Specifically, during periods when inflation and interest rates rise, high-dividend stocks may be particularly vulnerable. Public utility common stocks are a good example. Although they are known as low-beta stocks, they are likely to have high systematic risk with respect to interest rates and inflation. This is so not only because they are good substitutes for fixed-income securities, but also because public utilities are vulnerable to a profits squeeze during periods of rising inflation because of regulatory lags and increased borrowing costs. Hence, the

6. For corporate investors, 85 percent of dividend income is excluded from taxable income while capital gains are taxed at normal gains rates.

yield-tilted index fund with beta equal to one may not mirror the market index when inflation accelerates.

The actual experience of yield-tilted index funds during the 1979–80 period was far from reassuring. The performance of these funds was significantly worse than that of the market. Of course, we should not reject a model simply because of its failure over any specific short-term period. Nevertheless, I believe that an understanding of the wider aspects of systematic risk, such as provided here, would have helped prevent what turned out to be (at least over the short term) some serious investment errors.

Conclusion

I have argued here that no single measure is likely to capture adequately the variety of systematic risk influences on individual stocks and portfolios. Returns are sensitive to general market swings, to changes in interest rates and in the rate of inflation, to changes in National Income and, undoubtedly, to other economic factors as well. Moreover, if one were to select the best individual risk estimate, the traditional beta measure would probably not be our first choice. The dispersion of analysts' forecasts seems to have a closer relationship with expected returns and may be the best single measure of systematic risk available.

References

Ibbotson, Roger G., and Sinquefield, Rex A. 1979. Stocks, Bonds, Bills, and Inflation: Historical Returns (1926–1978). Financial Analysts Research Foundation, University of Virginia, Charlottesville.

Malkiel, Burton G., and Cragg, John G. 1980. Expectations and the Valuation of Shares. NBER Working Paper No. 471, Cambridge, MA. April.

Roll, Richard. 1977. A Critique of the Asset Pricing Theory's Tests. Part I: On Past and Potential Testability of the Theory. *Journal of Financial Economics* 4 (March): 129–76.

Ross, Stephen. 1976. The Arbitrage Theory of Capital Asset Pricing. *Journal of Economic Theory* 13 (December): 341–60.

3 Investment Strategy in an Inflationary Environment

Zvi Bodie

The basic premise of this chapter is that ultimately what is of concern to an investor, whether a household or an institutional investor such as a life insurance company or a pension fund, is the real value of its investments in terms of purchasing power over consumer goods and services. The issue to be addressed is what investment strategies make sense in an economic environment in which a major factor (although certainly not the only one) to be considered is substantial uncertainty about the future level of the prices of those goods and services. By investment strategy I mean decisions about how to allocate investable funds among four major asset classes: common stocks and other equity investments; long-term, fixed-interest debt instruments; short-term or variable-rate debt instruments; and other "inflation-hedging" assets such as commodity futures contracts or commodity-linked bonds.

The chapter is organized as follows. I will first discuss why it is real or inflation-adjusted rates of return and their uncertainty which ought to be the main concern of investors. I will then present an analytical framework for formulating investment strategy, examine the historical record of real rates of return on the four asset categories, and derive estimates of alternative risk-return tradeoff curves. Finally, I will discuss the implications of my findings for individual and institutional asset allocation policies.

Zvi Bodie is Professor of Economics and Finance at Boston University's School of Management and Co-Director of the NBER project on the economics of the U.S. pension system.

The author wishes to thank his colleague, Alex Kane, and his research assistant, Michael Rouse, for their valuable help in preparing this chapter.

3.1 Why It Is Real Investment Returns and Their Uncertainty That Matter

With respect to the individual investor, i.e., the household, there can be little doubt that the dollar value of its investment portfolio is not what counts, but rather its real value in terms of purchasing power. It follows, therefore, that households will be concerned about the real or inflation-adjusted rate of return rather than the nominal rate of return on their investments. If the future rate of inflation were known with certainty, it would make no difference whether households were making their portfolio decisions on the basis of real or nominal rates of return. The expected real rate on any particular asset would just be the nominal rate less the known inflation rate, and its real risk would be the same as its nominal risk. But in an environment of uncertainty about future inflation there can be a great difference between the real and nominal risk associated with an asset. The most extreme example is the case of conventional bonds and mortgages, which offer a guaranteed nominal return to an investor, but a highly uncertain real one. As inflation becomes more certain, these instruments become riskier and less attractive to households.

But what about institutional investors? Should they be concerned with real or nominal rates of return? Institutional investors are financial intermediaries between the nonfinancial business sector and the household sector of the economy. Their ultimate survival and success depend on providing households with the kinds of financial assets that households want to hold. In our inflationary environment contractual savings plans such as ordinary life insurance policies, which offer guaranteed nominal cash flows, and money-fixed annuities have become unattractive. In order to maintain their viability, life insurance companies must respond by offering new products and adjusting their investment policies accordingly. Elsewhere I have discussed the feasibility of indexed annuities as a possible innovation for providing stable real retirement income in an inflationary environment, and many other suggestions along these lines are bound to be forthcoming in the future. (Bodie 1980). The central concern of investment policy in this new environment will surely be real rates of return and their uncertainty.

What about pension plans and pension funds? Why should they care about real rates of return? Under many corporate defined-benefit pension plans, the starting level of the retirement benefit promised to the worker is based on an average of the worker's wage in the last several years prior to retirement. If, as in the past, wages increase in tandem with consumer prices, then such a plan's liabilities are in effect indexed during the phase of benefit accrual. Furthermore, it is likely that the future evolution of pension plans is going to be in the direction of at least partial indexation of benefits in the postretirement phase too. Thus, at least these pension funds have to plan their investment strategy with a focus on real rates of return too.

3.2   The Theory of Portfolio Selection

The analytical framework which underlies the investment strategies I will present in this chapter is known as mean-variance analysis, and it goes back almost thirty years to the pioneering work by Markowitz (1952). The basic premise underlying this approach is that the investor is risk averse; that is to say, given a choice between two investments offering the same mean (or average) rate of return, the investor always chooses the one that has less risk. Risk in the context of this analysis is identified with the unpredictability or uncertainty of achieving one's expected rate of return and is measured by its variance or standard deviation.

The investor's decision process is divided into two stages. In the first stage he computes what his risk-return opportunities are, and in the second he chooses the risk-return combination which suits him best. In stage one, the investor starts by finding the minimum-risk strategy, determining the mean rate of return associated with it, and then proceeding to derive other portfolios which offer higher and higher means with the least possible risk. The result of this part of the process is a tradeoff curve showing the terms-of-trade between risk and expected return.[1]

The inputs needed to generate the tradeoff curve are the means and standard deviations of the real rates of return on the individual assets and the correlations among them. In the following section we examine what these parameters have been over the past twenty-seven years and discuss our assumptions about their current values.

3.3   Inflation and Asset Returns: The Historical Record

Table 3.1 contains the historical record of real pretax rates of return on each of four categories of assets for the period 1953 through 1979. The measure of the price level that was used in adjusting these rates of return was the Personal Consumption Expenditures Deflator published by the U.S. Department of Commerce. This measure was chosen rather than the Department of Labor's Consumer Price Index (CPI) because serious doubts about the adequacy of the CPI as a measure of true inflation have been raised in the past seven or eight years. The main objection to the CPI is that it gives too much weight to new mortgage rates in the computation of shelter costs. The last two columns in Table 3.1 present the rate of inflation as measured first by the Consumer Price Index, then

---

1. For a discussion of how to choose the optimal point on the tradeoff curve see Bodie (1979).

Table 3.1   **Annual Real Rates of Return, 1953–79 (Percent per Year)**

	(1) Bills	(2) Bonds	(3) Stocks	(4) Commodity Futures	Rate of Inflation (5) CPI	(6) PCE Deflator
1953	0.43	2.22	−2.34	−3.46	0.62	1.38
1954	0.44	6.74	51.98	13.24	−0.50	0.42
1955	0.35	−2.49	29.97	−7.63	0.37	1.22
1956	−0.96	−8.74	3.01	12.38	2.86	3.45
1957	0.10	4.28	−13.41	−5.04	3.02	3.04
1958	0.37	−7.19	41.70	−3.47	1.76	1.17
1959	0.86	−4.24	9.68	−2.84	1.50	2.07
1960	1.20	12.16	0.96	−3.93	1.48	1.69
1961	0.90	−0.25	25.36	0.02	0.67	1.22
1962	1.02	5.11	−10.25	−2.40	1.22	1.69
1963	1.57	−0.32	20.95	16.32	1.65	1.53
1964	2.27	2.24	15.05	4.54	1.19	1.24
1965	1.33	−1.81	9.63	5.13	1.92	2.57
1966	2.09	1.00	−12.36	9.70	3.35	2.62
1967	0.53	−12.40	19.60	−0.06	3.04	3.66
1968	1.11	−4.14	6.74	−3.18	4.72	4.05
1969	1.44	−9.66	−12.92	12.19	6.11	5.07
1970	2.14	7.48	−0.28	−1.62	5.49	4.30
1971	0.34	8.83	9.87	−1.65	3.36	4.04
1972	0.14	1.92	14.75	29.35	3.41	3.69
1973	−2.21	−9.57	−21.96	72.69	8.80	9.35
1974	−1.99	−5.30	−33.28	17.97	12.20	10.19
1975	0.21	3.42	29.95	−10.03	7.01	5.58
1976	−0.43	10.63	17.35	5.31	4.81	5.53
1977	−0.76	−6.22	−12.37	4.90	6.77	5.92
1978	−1.07	−6.62	−1.66	18.61	9.03	8.19
1979	0.08	−10.44	7.39	15.59	13.31	10.29
Mean	0.43	−0.87	7.08	7.13	4.04	3.89
Std. Dev.	1.14	6.86	19.46	16.26	3.56	2.85

Correlation Coefficients:

	Bonds	Stocks	Commodity Futures	Inflation (PCE)
Bills	.357	.287	−.521	−.658
Bonds		.170	−.359	−.423
Stocks			−.333	−.527
Commodity futures				.532
Inflation (CPI)				.977

The real returns were calculated according to the formula:

$$\text{Real rate of return} = 100 \times \left(\frac{1 + \text{nominal rate of return}}{1 + \text{rate of inflation}} - 1 \right)$$

using the PCE Deflator inflation rate. The rate of return on commodity futures in column 4 was calculated differently, as explained in the text.

SOURCES: The data on 1-month bills, 20-year bonds, and stocks are from Ibbotson and Sinquefield (1977), updated by the authors. The commodity futures series was derived from price data in the *Wall Street Journal* using a method explained in the text. The data on the CPI and the PCE deflator are from U.S. Department of Labor and Department of Commerce, respectively.

as measured by the Personal Consumption Expenditures Deflator. There are serious differences between the two series, especially in 1974 and 1979; but as the correlation coefficient of .977 reported at the bottom of Table 3.1 indicates, they are highly positively correlated.

The first column in Table 3.1 is the real rate of return on a policy of "rolling over" thirty-day Treasury bills, and is representative of the rate of return on money market instruments. This is by far the least volatile series, with a standard deviation of only 1.14 percent. This is because over this period, short-term interest rates have tended to follow rather closely movements in the rate of inflation.

Of course, this is not a coincidence. All market-determined interest rates contain an "inflation premium," which reflects expectations about the declining purchasing power of the money borrowed over the life of the loan. As the rate of inflation has increased in recent years, so too has the inflation premium built into interest rates. While long-term as well as short-term interest rates contain such a premium, conventional long-term bonds lock the investor into the current interest rate for the life of the bond. If long-term interest rates on new bonds subsequently rise as a result of unexpected inflation, the funds already locked in can be released only by selling the bonds on the secondary market at a price well below their face value. But if an investor buys only short-term bonds with an average maturity of about thirty days, then the interest rate he earns will lag behind changes in the inflation rate by at most one month.

The problem with money market instruments, however, is their low rate of return. Over the past twenty-seven years, the average pretax, inflation-adjusted rate of return on money market instruments has been barely half a percent per year. In the most recent six-year period, that return has actually been negative. Perhaps the most likely scenario for the future is that inflation-adjusted returns will hover around zero, i.e., the interest rate will be about equal to the rate of inflation.

Column 2 presents the real rate of return an investor would have earned by investing in U.S. Treasury bonds with a twenty-year maturity. The assumption underlying this series is that the investor bought a twenty-year bond at the beginning of each year and sold it at the end. His return therefore includes both coupon interest and capital gains or losses. As the relatively low mean and high standard deviation indicate, the past twenty-seven years was a bad period for the investor in long-term bonds. Capital losses caused by unanticipated increases in interest rates usually more than cancelled the coupon yield over this period.

It would probably be a mistake to assume that the mean real rate of return on long-term government bonds in the future is going to be the $-.87\%$ per year that it was over the 1953 to 1979 period. A more reasonable approach to estimating the ex ante mean real rate would be to take the yield to maturity on long-term government bonds and subtract an estimate of the mean rate of inflation expected to prevail over the next twenty years. When we do this we find a mean real rate of return on U.S. Treasury bonds of 2% per year.

Column 3 in Table 3.1 presents the real rate of return on the Standard and Poor's Composite Index of common stocks, which is a value-weighted stock portfolio of the five hundred largest corporations in the United States. The return includes dividends and capital gains. The mean real rate over our sample period was 7.08% per year, but we will use 10% per year as our estimate of the ex ante mean in our computations of the tradeoff curve. There are two main reasons for doing so. The first is that several recent careful studies of the real rate of return on unlevered corporate capital (i.e., the return to debt and equity combined) indicate it to be in the range of 6 to 7% per year (Brainard, Shoven, and Weiss 1980; Feldstein and Summers 1977; Holland and Myers 1977). Since the average debt-equity ratio for the S&P 500 companies is about ⅓, and the after-tax real interest rate on corporate borrowing is quite negative, a 10% mean real rate of return on levered equity seems plausible.[2] The second reason is that 10% per year is the estimate of the mean real rate of return on the S&P 500 derived by Merton (1980) in a recent National Bureau of Economic Research study employing a new estimation technique, which incorporates more information than just the simple average of past rates.

Finally, let us focus our attention on column 4 in Table 3.1, which presents the annual rate of return one would have earned on a well-diversified portfolio of commodity futures contracts over the 1953 to 1979 period. The rate of return on a futures contract reflects the proportional change in the futures price over the holding period. The series was generated by assuming a "buy-and-hold" strategy whereby contracts were entered into at quarterly intervals, held for three months, and then liquidated. The number of commodities increases from thirteen in 1953 to twenty-two by the end of the period. Table 3.2 presents the list of commodities and the year in which each was added to the portfolio. The portfolio was assumed to consist of equal dollar amounts invested in each commodity contract.

The rates of return for commodity futures listed in column 4 of Table 3.1 require a different interpretation than the real rates in columns 1 through 3. When an investor takes a long position in a futures contract, he

2. The relationship between the rate of return on levered equity (ROE), the rate of return on total capital (ROC), the after-tax interest rate on debt (I), and the debt/equity ratio is given by the formula:

$$ROE = ROC + (ROC - I)\frac{\text{Debt}}{\text{Equity}}$$

Assuming a 15% per year nominal interest rate on corporate debt, a 50% tax rate, and a 12% per year expected rate of inflation, we get a real after-tax interest rate on the debt of -4.5% per year. Substituting this value into the formula for I, 6.5% per year for ROC, and ⅓ for the debt/equity ratio, we find that $ROE \simeq 10\%$ per year.

Table 3.2   **List of Commodity Futures Contracts Included in the Portfolio**

Commodity	Year of Entrance into the Portfolio	Commodity	Year of Entrance into the Portfolio
Wheat	1953	Copper	1953
Corn	1953	Sugar	1953
Oats	1953	Silver	1963
Soybeans	1953	Cattle	1964
Soybean oil	1953	Platinum	1964
Soybean meal	1953	Pork bellies	1964
Potatoes	1953	Hogs	1966
Wool	1953	Orange juice	1966
Cotton	1953	Broilers	1968
Eggs	1953	Lumber	1969
Cocoa	1953	Plywood	1970

does not buy it in the sense that he would buy a stock or bond or the physical commodity itself; rather, he agrees to purchase the commodity for a specified price at a certain point in the future. The commodities exchange, which acts as an intermediary, requires all parties to a futures contract to post a bond called "margin" to guarantee performance.[3] Investors are permitted to post Treasury bills, on which they continue to earn the interest, so the funds used as margin are therefore not strictly speaking an investment in commodity futures. The rates of return reported in column 4 should therefore be interpreted as the addition to the total investment portfolio rate of return that the investor would have earned in each year had he taken a position in commodity futures with a face value equal to his total investment in other assets.

In order for a buy-and-hold strategy in the futures market to be profitable, it is not enough for spot prices to be rising; they must rise by more than was anticipated in the futures price at the time the contract was entered into. On average, one might expect the spot price forecasts implicit in futures prices to be right, and therefore expect the mean rate of return on futures contracts to be zero.[4] But what is more important for our purposes, futures contracts will yield a positive rate of return when there are *unanticipated* increases in spot prices, and it is this feature which makes them valuable as an inflation hedge.

The critical parameters which determine how valuable commodity futures are in this role, and which play a crucial role in determining the shape of the tradeoff curve, are the correlation coefficients presented at the bottom of Table 3.1. Perhaps the most significant thing to notice is

3. Margins on commodity figures contracts are typically quite low, ranging from 7 to 10 percent of the face value of the contract. For more detail about the commodity futures series see Bodie and Rosanksy (1980).

4. There is a good deal of controversy in the economics literature on this point. For further discussion and references see Bodie and Rosansky (1980).

that the real rates of return on bills, bonds, and stocks are all negatively correlated with inflation and all positively correlated with each other. But commodity futures are positively correlated with the rate of inflation and negatively correlated with the real rates of return on the other major asset categories, and therefore can serve to reduce the risk associated with any portfolio containing them.

The mean rate of return on our buy-and-hold strategy in commodity futures during the 1953 to 1979 period was 7.13% per year, a strikingly large number, and one which may not be an accurate indicator for the future. In computing the tradeoff curve we will assume a mean of zero, although we will also discuss the consequences of assuming a higher value.

Before proceeding to our presentation of the risk-return tradeoff curves in the next section, let us summarize the assumptions that we are making about the key parameters relating to the real rates of return on bills, bonds, stocks, and commodity futures and the interrelationships among them. With regard to the means, we assume zero on bills, 2% on bonds, 10% on stocks, and zero on commodity futures. With regard to the standard deviations and correlations we assume the ones reported in Table 3.1.

3.4   The Risk-Return Tradeoff

We will begin our analysis of the risk-return tradeoff by looking at portfolios consisting only of stocks and bills. The minimum-risk investment strategy is to invest entirely in bills, in which case one's mean real rate of return would be zero and one's standard deviation 1.14%. At the other extreme one could invest everything in stocks, in which case the mean real rate of return on the portfolio would be 10% and the standard deviation 19.46%. Table 3.3 shows us the combinations of mean and standard deviation of real rate of return an investor would achieve by going from one of these extremes to the other.[5] Figure 3.1 graphs this tradeoff curve as curve 1. For mean values above 1% per year, curve 1 is very close to a straight line with a slope of .53, indicating an increase of about two percentage points in standard deviation for every one percentage point increase in mean.

---

5. The formula for computing the standard deviation of the real rate of return on any portfolio consisting of stocks and bills is:

$$SD_p^2 = (1 - X)^2 \, SD_b^2 + X^2 \, SD_s^2 + 2X(1 - X)R \, SD_b \, SD_s$$

where SD_b and SD_s represent the standard deviations on bills and stocks, respectively, and R the correlation coefficient between them. X is the proportion of the portfolio invested in stocks, and therefore $1 - X$ is the proportion invested in bills.

Table 3.3   **Risk-Return Tradeoff Curve: Stocks and Bills**

Mean	Std. Dev.	Slope	Portfolio Proportions	
			Stocks	Bills
0%	1.14%		0	1.0
		.77		
1	2.44		.1	.9
		.56		
2	4.24		.2	.8
		.53		
3	6.11		.3	.7
		.53		
4	8.00		.4	.6
		.52		
5	9.91		.5	.5
		.52		
6	11.81		.6	.4
		.52		
7	13.72		.7	.3
		.52		
8	15.63		.8	.2
		.52		
9	17.54		.9	.1
		.52		
10	19.46		1.0	0

Assumptions about real rates of return:

	Bills	Stocks
Mean	0%	10.0%
Std. Dev.	1.14%	19.46%

Correlation Coefficients:

Stocks	.287

In order to provide a clearer picture of the meaning of a movement along the risk-return tradeoff curve, we have graphed in Figure 3.2 three probability distributions, corresponding to the first three points on curve 1. They are based on the assumption that the distribution of the real rate of return on the portfolios is normal, i.e., a "bell-shaped" curve. The first corresponds to the portfolio consisting of bills only, which has a mean of zero and a standard deviation of 1.14%; the second, to the portfolio which has 90 percent invested in bills and ten percent invested in stocks with a mean real rate of return of 1% per year and a standard deviation of 2.44%; and the third, to a portfolio which has eighty percent invested in bills, twenty percent in stocks with a mean of 2% per year and a standard deviation of 4.24%. As the proportion of the portfolio invested in stocks and therefore the mean go up, the bell-shaped curve shifts to the right and becomes more flat or stretched out, indicating greater upside potential but also greater downside risk.

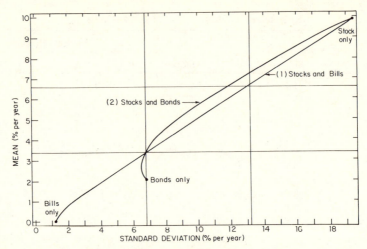

Fig. 3.1   Risk-Return Tradeoff Curves.

Now let us consider what the tradeoff curve would look like if the investor were restricted to combinations of bonds and stocks. This curve is tabulated in Table 3.4 and graphed as curve 2 in Figure 3.1. Note that as we move up curve 2 from a bonds-only portfolio to one containing a little stock, the standard deviation actually falls a bit before starting to grow. The minimum-risk stock-bond portfolio contains 6.4% stocks and 93.6% bonds and has a mean and standard deviation of 2.51% per year and 6.64%, respectively.[6] This implies that no risk-averse investor would ever rationally choose to hold a bonds-only portfolio, since by substituting a small amount of stock for some of the bonds, he could both increase his expected rate of return and reduce his risk.

As a comparison of curves 1 and 2 makes clear, at mean real rates of return greater then 3.5%, the stock-bond portfolios have less risk for any mean than do the corresponding stock-bill portfolios. On the other hand, for mean values below 3.5%, stock-bill portfolios have less risk for any mean than do the corresponding stock-bond portfolios. Perhaps more important, however, is the fact that very low risk strategies are unattainable using only stocks and bonds. The minimum-risk stock-bond portfolio still has a standard deviation of 6.64%, which is quite high compared with the lower risk levels attainable with bills.

6. The formula for finding the minimum-risk proportion of stocks is:

$$X_{\min} = \frac{SD_b^2 - RSD_bSD_s}{SD_b^2 + SD_s^2 - 2RSD_bSD_s}$$

Note that when we combine bills with stocks, this formula yields a negative number for the proportion of stocks, which means we would actually have to sell some stock short in order to minimize risk. This explains why curve 1 in Figure 3.1 does not have the same shape as curve 2 at its lower end.

Table 3.4   **Risk-Return Tradeoff Curve: Stocks and Bonds**

| | | | Portfolio Proportions ||
Mean	Std. Dev.	Slope	Stocks	Bonds
2%	6.86%		0	1.0
		−5.88		
3	6.85		.125	.875
		1.45		
4	7.66		.25	.75
		.71		
5	9.07		.375	.625
		.49		
6	10.85		.5	.5
		.50		
7	12.85		.625	.375
		.47		
8	14.98		.75	.25
		.45		
9	17.19		.875	.125
		.44		
10	19.46		1.0	0

Assumptions about real rates of return:

	Bonds	Stocks
Mean	2%	10.0%
Std. Dev.	6.86%	19.46%

Correlation Coefficients:

Stocks	.170

The minimum-risk portfolio consists of 6.4 percent stocks and 93.6 percent bonds and has a mean and standard deviation of 2.51 percent and 6.64 percent, respectively.

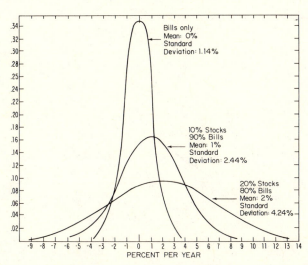

Fig. 3.2   Probability Distributions of Bill and Stock Portfolios.

Table 3.5   **Risk-Return Tradeoff Curve: Stocks, Bills, and Bonds**

Mean	Std. Dev.	Slope	Portfolio Proportions		
			Stocks	Bonds	Bills
0%	1.14%		0	0	1.00
		.84			
1	2.33		.08	.10	.82
		.62			
2	3.94		.15	.22	.63
		.59			
3	5.63		.23	.33	.44
		.58			
4	7.34		.31	.45	.24
		.58			
5	9.06		.39	.56	.05
		.56			
6	10.85		.50	.50	0
		.50			
7	12.85		.63	.37	0
		.47			
8	14.98		.75	.25	0
		.45			
9	17.19		.88	.12	0
		.44			
10	19.46		1.00	0	0

Assumptions about real rates of return:

	Bills	Bonds	Stocks
Mean	0%	2%	10%
Std. Dev.	1.14%	6.86%	19.46%

Correlation Coefficients:

Bonds	.357	
Stocks	.287	.170

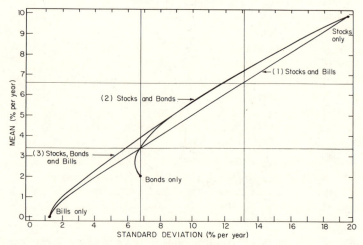

Fig. 3.3   Risk-Return Tradeoff Curves.

Now let us consider portfolios containing all three assets: stocks, bonds, and bills. The process of computing the tradeoff curve in this case is more complicated than before, because for each value of mean real rate of return, one must use an optimization procedure to find that portfolio which has the lowest standard deviation (Markowitz 1952). The resulting tradeoff curve and portfolio proportions are presented in Table 3.5 and Figure 3.3, which allows us to compare the risk-return tradeoff curve derived using all three assets with the two previously derived curves from Figure 3.1.

The main improvement comes at the low-risk, low-return end of the curve. The minimum-risk strategy is still to invest in bills only, but as we move up the curve we replace bills with increasing amounts of both bonds and stocks. This continues up to a mean of 5% per year. At higher means bills disappear from the portfolio, and the proportion of bonds declines; curve 3 just becomes identical to curve 2. One point of special interest on curve 3, which is not tabulated in Table 3.5, is the point having the same mean as the minimum-risk stock-bond portfolio on curve 2, i.e., 2.5% per year. It consists of a portfolio with 53% bills, 28% bonds, and 19% stocks and has a standard deviation of 4.78%, as opposed to the 6.64% standard deviation of the minimum-risk stock-bond portfolio. Thus by adding bills to the minimum-risk stock-bond portfolio one can achieve a substantial reduction in risk with no loss in expected return.

Now we are ready to introduce commodity futures contracts into our portfolio. It is important to remember that when we take a position in commodity futures we are not actually using up any of our funds; our funds are invested in stocks, bonds, and bills. We are simply taking a position which has a face value equal to some specified proportion of the total amount invested in these other assets. The only restriction on our portfolio imposed by the futures contracts is that we must have an amount invested in bills equal to at least 10% of the position in commodity futures, to serve as margin.

The results with commodity futures included are presented in Table 3.6 and Figure 3.4. Note that the minimum-risk strategy is still to invest 100% of our funds in bills, but it is now optimal to hedge that investment with a small position in our well-diversified commodity futures portfolio by taking a long position with a face value equal to 4% of the investment in bills. Under our assumption that the mean rate of return on commodity futures is zero, the mean real rate of return on our portfolio will remain unaffected, but there will be a reduction in standard deviation.

Comparing curves 3 and 4 in Figure 3.4, we see that for any mean real rate of return, introducing the right amount of commodity futures contracts into our portfolio enables us to reduce our standard deviation by a significant amount. The reduction in standard deviation increases steadily the higher the mean value, and is at its greatest value at a mean of 9% per year. Introducing commodity futures shifts the tradeoff curve to the

Table 3.6   **Risk-Return Tradeoff: Stocks, Bonds, Bills, and Commodity Futures**

Mean	Std. Dev.	Slope	Portfolio Proportions			
			Stocks	Bonds	Bills	Commodity Futures
0%	0.97%		0	0	1.00	.04
		1.01				
1	1.96		.08	.12	.80	.08
		.67				
2	3.44		.15	.24	.61	.12
		.65				
3	4.99		.23	.37	.41	.16
		.63				
4	6.57		.30	.49	.21	.20
		.63				
5	8.16		.38	.59	.03	.24
		.56				
6	9.93		.51	.46	.03	.27
		.50				
7	11.93		.63	.34	.03	.29
		.47				
8	14.06		.76	.21	.03	.32
		.45				
9	16.26		.88	.08	.04	.34
		.33				
10	19.46		1.00	0	0	0

Assumptions about real rates of return:

	Bills	Bonds	Stocks	Commodity Futures
Mean	0%	2.0%	10.0%	0%
Std. Dev.	1.14%	6.86%	19.46%	16.26%
Correlation Coefficients:				
Bonds	.357			
Stocks	.287	.170		
Commodity futures	−.521	−.359	−.333	

left by .17% at the minimum-risk end of the curve and by .93% at the other end.

Looking at the last four columns in Table 3.6 and comparing them with the last three columns of Table 3.5, we see that the addition of commodity futures contracts does not change the portfolio proportions of stocks, bonds, and bills by much. The major effect is that bills no longer disappear entirely from the portfolio as they did before when we moved to high mean real rates of return, because now there is a need for bills to serve as margin on the commodity futures contracts. We also see that as we move to higher mean real rates of return and the investment in stocks goes up, there is a steady increase in the size of the relative position in commodity futures, although it never exceeds 34 percent of the total value of the investment portfolio.

What is the effect on the tradeoff curve of assuming a positive mean rate of return on commodity futures? Table 3.7 and Figure 3.5 present the

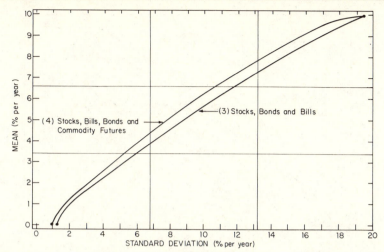

Fig. 3.4   Risk-Return Tradeoff Curves.

results of assuming a 2% per year mean rate. Perhaps the best way to describe the effect is as an upward shift of the entire curve. At any level of risk it becomes possible to achieve a higher mean real rate of return, with the gain being larger the higher the level of risk. Even the minimum-risk portfolio now has a positive mean rate of return. It now becomes possible to attain a 10% mean real rate of return with a standard deviation of only 16.39% instead of 19.46%, by holding a portfolio consisting of 86% stocks, 8% bonds, 6% bills, and a position in commodity futures equal to 59% of the portfolio's value.

It should be stressed once again before ending this part of the chapter that the role of commodity futures stems from the fact that it is the only asset whose returns are positively correlated with inflation. The reason

Table 3.7   **Effect of Increased Mean Rate of Return on Commodity Futures to 2 Percent per Year**

Mean	Std. Dev.	Portfolio Proportions			
		Stocks	Bonds	Bills	Commodity Futures
0.1%	.97%	0	0	1.00	.04
1.0	1.74	.06	.10	.84	.09
2	3.06	.13	.21	.66	.14
3	4.46	.19	.33	.48	.20
4	5.89	.26	.44	.30	.25
5	7.32	.33	.55	.12	.31
6	8.81	.41	.55	.04	.36
7	10.53	.53	.43	.04	.41
8	12.40	.64	.31	.05	.47
9	14.37	.75	.19	.06	.53
10	16.39	.86	.08	.06	.59

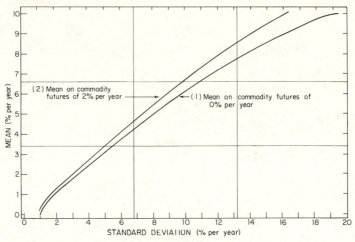

Fig. 3.5   Risk-Return Tradeoff Curves

the proportion of commodity futures in the portfolio rises in Table 3.6 as the investment in stocks goes up is that the real return on stocks is negatively correlated with inflation. I have performed the experiment of deriving the tradeoff curve under the assumption that the real return on stocks is uncorrelated with inflation, and the result is that there would be virtually no role for commodity futures contracts in that case. It is their value as a hedge against inflation, to offset the inflation risk associated with the investment in stocks, that accounts for commodity futures' significant role.

3.5   Implications of Findings for Asset Allocation

The first implication of our findings is that bills are the cornerstone of any low-risk investment strategy. Here it is important to keep in mind that bills for us are a proxy for all money market instruments and floating rate debt. Our results indicate that in order to achieve a low degree of risk, by which we mean a standard deviation below 4%, at least half of the portfolio would have to be invested in these securities. Of course, along with the low risk comes a low return.

Who might be interested in a low-risk strategy, despite its low return? The prime candidates are probably retired people with a small-to-moderate accumulation of assets and a low tolerance for risk. In Great Britain the government has for years been selling bonds bearing a zero real interest rate on a voluntary and restricted basis to citizens aged sixty-five and over. These bonds have proven to be a very popular investment.

Our findings carry two important messages to institutional investors such as life insurance companies. The first is that households can currently provide themselves with a fairly safe pretax real rate of return of about zero by investing in money market funds. Therefore any new kind of contractual savings plan would have to offer a similar rate. The second is that if the insurance industry wanted to offer savings plans and/or annuities with full or partial indexation they could hedge almost all of the investment risk by investing primarily in money market instruments. In fact, if they wanted to avoid the investment risk altogether, they could offer them as variable annuities.

What can we say about the role of bonds and other long-term fixed interest securities? The first point suggested by our findings is that one can get along without bonds with very little loss of portfolio efficiency; the improvement in the risk-return tradeoff that one gets from adding bonds to stocks and bills is relatively minor. Some institutional portfolio managers might say that the risk associated with long-term bonds is exaggerated in my findings because I have included in my measure of annual returns unrealized capital gains and losses. Most insurance companies and pension funds do not count unrealized capital gains or losses on long-term bonds as part of their annual rate of return. But even if we disregard them, any instrument which commits the investor to a fixed nominal flow of coupon income and a money-fixed principal amount at maturity is in fact extremely risky even for an investor with a long-run horizon, in fact, especially for such an investor.

Many institutional investors have already come to the conclusion that long-term fixed interest securities are too risky relative to their expected return and have simply stopped investing in them. If that trend continues we can expect to see the disappearance of these financial instruments from the U.S. capital market. In Great Britain the market for long-term fixed interest corporate debt disappeared rather quickly in 1974 and has not reappeared since. If this market is to maintain its viability in the U.S., the mean real rate of return will have to be higher than in the past.

Finally, what are the implications of our findings for investments in commodity futures contracts or other inflation-hedging assets? Our results indicate that as long as stocks are negatively correlated with inflation, there is going to be a need for some kind of asset that has the property that its rate of return is positively correlated with inflation. Commodity futures contracts have the considerable advantage of already being in existence and therefore can be used right away.

There are some new types of financial instruments that have started to appear and may play an increasingly significant role in this regard in the future. I am referring specifically to commodity-linked bonds, that is to say, bonds whose principal and/or interest is linked to the price of some commodity. The silver-linked bonds issued by the Sunshine Mining Corporation are an example. Bonds linked to the price of petroleum and other natural resources owned by the issuing corporation are being actively discussed by the institutional investment community. These securities would share with commodity futures contracts the property that their rate of return would be positively correlated with the rate of inflation. If significant inflation persists in the future, these kinds of securities will probably come to play an important role in investment portfolios.

References

Bodie, Z. 1979. Hedging against Inflation. *Sloan Management Review*. Fall.

————. 1980. An Innovation for Stable Real Retirement Income. *Journal of Portfolio Management*. Fall.

Bodie, Z., and Rosansky, V. 1980. Risk and Return in Commodity Futures. *Financial Analysts Journal*. May/June.

Brainard, W. C.; Shoven, J. B.; and Weiss, L. 1980. The Financial Valuation of the Return to Capital. *Brookings Papers on Economic Activity* 2: 453–502.

Feldstein, M., and Summers, L. 1979. Is the Rate of Profit Falling? *Brookings Papers on Economic Activity* 1: 211–27.

Holland, D., and Myers, S. C. 1977. Trends in Corporate Profitability and Capital Costs. Sloan School of Management Working Paper. March.

Ibbotson, R., and Sinquefield, R. 1977. Stocks, Bonds, Bills, and Inflation: Historical Returns (1926–1978). Financial Analysts Research Foundation, University of Virginia, Charlottesville.

Markowitz, H. 1952. Portfolio Selection. *Journal of Finance*. March.

Merton, R. C. 1980. On Estimating the Expected Return on the Market: An Exploratory Investigation. *Journal of Financial Economics*. December.

4 Changing Balance Sheet Relationships in the U.S. Manufacturing Sector, 1926–77

John H. Ciccolo, Jr.

Several aspects of the recent performance of U.S. nonfinancial corporations have attracted widespread attention. Since the mid-1960s there has been a dramatic decline in the securities markets' valuation of these firms relative to the replacement costs of their assets, and also relative to the returns generated by these assets (Brainard, Shoven, and Weiss 1980; Feldstein 1980). At the same time, nonfinancial corporate businesses have become more reliant on debt securities in financing their growth. (Friedman 1980, pp. 21–26). The inflationary environment of the past fifteen years has provided a powerful incentive for those with taxable incomes to increase their indebtedness. Additionally, as Friedman (1980) points out, the postwar trend away from internal sources of funds toward debt financing represents, at least partially, an adjustment toward more normal pre-Depression debt levels.

To place these issues in perspective, this chapter documents trends in the sources and uses of funds, market valuations, and rates of return for a small sample of manufacturing corporations over the 1926–77 period. The emphasis of the study is on the detailed market valuations of the firms' securities. There are several advantages to this sampling approach. First, a consistent set of aggregate balance sheet and income accounts is unavailable for the prewar period. Also, by working at the individual firm level, one can obtain more accurate information on the market values of traded securities and more detailed information on the structure of firms' balance sheets than is typically available at the aggregate level. While the purpose of this chapter is to describe only the aggregate characteristics of this sample, future research will use the underlying micro data set to test

John H. Ciccolo, Jr., is Associate Professor of Economics at Boston College and a research associate of the National Bureau of Economic Research.

specific hypotheses regarding company financing and investment decisions, and the financial markets' valuation of these activities.

The sample of firms used in this study is actually composed of nine separate subsamples of firms drawn periodically from various editions of *Moody's Industrial Manual*. The composition of this sample is outlined in Table 4.1. The goal was to obtain subsamples of size fifty but, given our criteria regarding reporting and accounting procedures, this was not always possible. This procedure of using subsamples of firms has the advantage of admitting to the sample firms that were created or destroyed during the 1926–77 period, but presents some problems in maintaining continuity.

While fifty items relating to the income account, balance sheet, and market valuations of the firms are included in the data base, a substantial amount of aggregation is performed to present the general characteristics of the sample. Accordingly, the balance sheets of the sample firms are consolidated as described in Table 4.2. For each firm, variables of interest—such as new debt or equity issues—are measured relative to net assets. Then firm data are averaged for each year to provide a time series for a hypothetical firm with the mean characteristics of its subsample. Table 4.3 shows the results of performing such calculations on the components of net assets for the overlapping years of the subsamples as well as for the years 1926–27 and the years 1976–77.

An interesting feature of the results presented in Table 4.3 is the rather dramatic decline in the Cash Items variable, which is composed mainly of cash and short-term marketable securities. Considered in conjunction with the recent increase in the role of debt in corporate capital structure, the decline is even more striking. Closer inspection indicates that, at least since the mid-1960s, the fall in the share of Cash Items in net assets has been accompanied by an increase in the share of physical capital. The drastic jump in Current Liabilities in 1941 is due primarily to increased corporate taxation.

Table 4.1   Sample Description

Subsample Number	Years of Coverage	Volume of Moody's (Source)	Number of Firms in Subsample	Number of Years
1	1926–30	1931	48	5
2	1930–35	1936	46	6
3	1935–41	1942	48	7
4	1941–47	1948	47	7
5	1947–53	1954	50	7
6	1953–59	1960	50	7
7	1959–65	1966	47	7
8	1965–71	1972	37	7
9	1971–77	1978	40	7

Table 4.2	Typical Firm's Balance Sheet

Net Assets

Cash items
+ Receivables
+ Inventories (replacement)
+ Net Property (replacement)
− Current liabilities (excluding short-term debt)
+ Miscellaneous items (net)

Liabilities

Short-term debt
+ Traded long-term debt
+ Nontraded long-term debt
+ Preferred stock
+ Common stockholders' equity

Table 4.3	Composition of Net Assets, Selected Years (As a Percentage of Net Assets)

	Cash Items	Receivables	Inventories	Net Property	Current Liabilities	Miscellaneous
1926–27	15.3	14.4	25.4	47.7	− 7.4	4.8
1930	18.0	11.2	22.2	48.2	− 6.1	6.6
1935	22.1	11.4	22.3	42.7	− 7.3	8.3
1941	22.8	14.6	31.3	43.2	− 20.5	7.7
1947	22.0	16.4	32.5	45.2	− 21.3	5.9
1953	24.7	16.1	33.6	47.5	− 26.2	4.4
1959	17.1	17.5	29.5	48.6	− 19.5	5.6
1965	13.4	20.1	30.8	47.0	− 21.9	6.6
1971	10.1	20.6	29.6	49.5	− 19.2	6.9
1976–77	10.2	19.4	26.3	53.0	− 20.9	6.4

Rows may not sum to 100 percent because of rounding.

4.1   Sources and Uses of Funds

Figure 4.1 illustrates the relative importance of external and internal funds in financing our "average" firm, while Figure 4.2 depicts the role of debt among external sources of finance. In both figures, the large spikes appearing above the years 1937, 1941, 1947, 1951, 1956, and 1974 coincide with periods of unusual inventory accumulation and apparently represent a demand for external funds to finance unplanned inventories. However, this is not true of the broad spike that appears above the years 1965–68. During this period there was an unusually large demand for funds for capital expenditures and for takeovers.[1]

1. Takeovers show up on the balance sheet in Miscellaneous Items as this variable contains the difference between the actual cost of an acquisition and its book value. Generally, acquisitions exceeding 10 percent of the purchasing firm's net assets disqualified the firm from the sample.

To highlight the longer-run trends, data on sources and uses of funds have been averaged over the individual years of the subsamples, and the results are presented in Table 4.4. According to these results, net issues of debt securities remained quite constant from the 1936–41 period to the mid-1960s, when a large shift toward external sources of funds occurred. In fact, the percentage of total sources accounted for by net debt issues

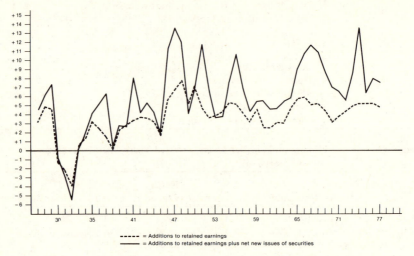

----- = Additions to retained earnings
—— = Additions to retained earnings plus net new issues of securities

Fig. 4.1   Sources of Funds as a Percentage of Net Assets, 1927–77.

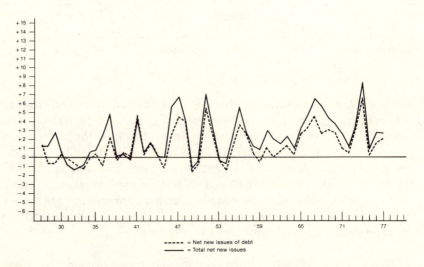

----- = Net new issues of debt
—— = Total net new issues

Fig. 4.2   Sources of External Funds as a Percentage of Net Assets, 1927–77.

Table 4.4   Sources and Uses of Funds as a Percentage of Net Assets

Sources

	Total Sources	Debt Issues	Debt Retirements	Stock[a] Issues	Stock Retirements	Undistributed Profits	CCA
1927–30	7.3	2.4	−2.3	2.1	−0.8	2.8	3.1
1931–35	2.6	0.9	−1.5	0.9	−0.9	−0.1	3.3
1936–41	7.5	2.4	−1.4	1.6	−0.6	2.2	3.3
1942–47	10.3	2.8	−1.5	2.0	−0.7	4.1	3.6
1948–53	11.0	2.9	−1.2	0.7	−0.7	5.4	3.5
1954–59	10.6	2.4	−1.4	1.5	−0.5	4.4	4.2
1960–65	10.6	2.6	−1.5	1.6	−0.4	3.6	4.7
1966–71	13.9	4.5	−1.5	2.1	−0.3	4.6	4.6
1972–77	12.5	4.8	−2.4	1.5	−0.6	4.9	4.3

Uses

	Total Uses	Plant/ Equipment	Cash Items	Inventories	Receivables	Misc. (Net)	Current Liabilities
1927–30	6.4	5.2	1.0	−0.2	−0.6	0.7	0.3
1931–35	2.5	2.5	0.3	0.1	−0.1	0.0	−0.3
1936–41	7.2	4.7	1.0	2.9	1.6	0.1	−3.1
1942–47	10.6	7.8	2.6	3.2	0.9	−1.8	−2.1
1948–53	10.9	7.4	2.1	2.7	1.3	−0.1	−2.5
1954–59	10.4	7.1	0.6	1.8	1.6	0.2	−0.9
1960–65	10.4	7.6	0.7	1.8	1.7	0.4	−1.8
1966–71	13.7	8.7	0.7	3.2	2.1	1.0	−2.0
1972–77	12.7	8.6	1.4	3.1	2.4	0.2	−3.0

[a]Both preferred and common shares.

since 1965 is about twenty, slightly more than double the pre-1965 percentage. The results of Table 4.4 also clearly illustrate the increased demand for funds to finance nonfinancial activities that has occurred since the mid-1960s. Virtually all of the jump in Total Uses is accounted for by increased expenditures on physical assets. The gradual trend toward external, relative to internal, sources of funds during the earlier postwar years reflects primarily a decline in undistributed profits relative to net assets.

Several features of the 1927–30 and 1931–35 periods require comment. First, during 1927–30 there were virtually no retirements of common stock, and the -0.8 figure under Stock Requirements is solely due to retirements of preferred stock. Net issues of common equity were negligible except for the years 1928 and 1929. Furthermore, the Plant/Equipment numbers for years prior to 1935 were estimated as depreciation allowances plus the change in net property account and are thus not comparable with the figures presented for later years. This latter feature of the data accounts for the relatively large discrepancy between Total Uses and Total Sources for 1927–30. Also, the relatively low number for Undistributed Profits for the 1927–30 period, 2.8 percent of net assets, is not indicative of low profitability, as seventy percent of funds available for common stock were paid out as dividends.

4.2   Market Valuations

Securities markets provide a continuing valuation of corporations and their earnings streams and, therefore, indirectly of their net assets. This section of the chapter investigates how these market valuations have behaved, relative to net assets, over the 1926–77 period.

Figure 4.3 plots the ratio of the market value of securities to net assets for each of the nine overlapping subsamples. In addition the diagram indicates the composition of the total ratio. For instance, the distance between the horizontal axis and the first broken line represents the market valuation of debt securities relative to net assets. To assist in interpreting the figure, Table 4.5 provides the average values for the overlapping years of the subsamples, as well as for 1926–27 and 1976–77.[2]

Both Table 4.5 and Figure 4.3 clearly indicate the increasing importance of debt in the capital structure of our "average" corporation. What is somewhat surprising is that the sum of debt and preferred stock, relative to net assets, has remained virtually constant over the entire fifty-year period, suggesting that the increase in debt has come primarily at the expense of preferred stock.

Another feature of Figure 4.3 which clearly stands out is the sharp fall and subsequent rapid recovery of the common equity component of the

2. Debt due in less than one year is valued at book. Nontraded long-term debt is valued using a bond price index generated for each year for each subsample.

Table 4.5   **Market Value of Securities Relative to Net Assets**

	Debt	Preferred	Common	Total	Debt Relative to Preferred + Common
1926–27	.123	.147	1.175	1.44	.093
1930	.091	.154	1.345	1.59	.061
1935	.068	.194	1.350	1.61	.044
1941	.076	.170	0.853	1.10	.074
1947	.099	.110	1.001	1.21	.089
1953	.132	.057	0.798	0.99	.154
1959	.140	.026	1.494	1.66	.092
1965	.156	.015	1.775	1.95	.087
1971	.202	.026	1.307	1.53	.152
1976–77	.205	.013	0.675	0.89	.298

ratio during the 1930–34 period. This is even more dramatic when one considers that capital goods prices were falling and, thus, reducing net assets and moving the ratio in the opposite direction.

Figure 4.3 also plainly shows the substantial decline in equity values that began in 1968. This slide in the ratio of the market value of equity relative to net assets is steeper and more prolonged than any previous decline illustrated in the diagram.

4.3   Rates of Return

This section presents calculations of several measures of the returns experienced by firms in the sample. Figure 4.4 compares the rate of

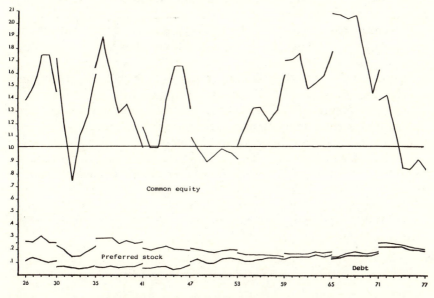

Fig. 4.3   Market Value of Securities Relative to Net Assets, 1926–77.

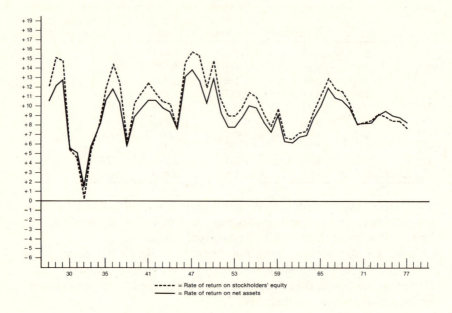

= Rate of return on stockholders' equity
= Rate of return on net assets

Fig. 4.4   Net Rates of Return, 1927–77.

return on common stockholders' equity with the total rate of return on net assets. In computing both rates, an adjustment is made to put depreciation charges on a replacement basis. Stockholders' equity is defined here as net assets minus the market values of debt and preferred stock.[3] An inventory valuation adjustment (IVA) is not included in the numbers in Figure 4.4 as, to date, the data base contains information sufficient to compute the IVA only for the years since 1960. However, an IVA is included in Table 4.6 which compares various rates of return computed for the 1961–70 and 1971–77 periods. Coupled with the information presented in Figure 4.3 and Table 4.5, these results confirm the significant decline which has recently occurred in the securities markets' valuation of assets relative to the returns generated by these assets. When we consider the differences in samples, the rates of return on net assets, inclusive of the IVA, are surprisingly close to those reported by Brainard, Shoven, and Weiss (1980, Table 1, p. 463). Their estimates for the rate of return on net assets are 7.8 and 6.9 percent for the 1961–70 and 1971–77 periods, respectively, compared with the estimates of 8.7 and 7.5 percent presented in Table 4.6.

3. Analogous calculations using book values have little effect on the results.

Table 4.6   **Rates of Return (Percent)**

	Rates of Return on Stockholders' Equity		Rates of Return on Net Assets	
	With IVA	Without IVA	With IVA	Without IVA
1961–70	9.3	9.7	8.7	9.1
1971–77	6.3	8.6	7.5	9.0

The rates of return reported in Table 4.6 ignore the effects of inflation and expected inflation on the real value of the firms' financial assets and liabilities. In particular, the component of the rate of return on net assets which reflects the tax deductibility of the inflation premium contained in nominal interest rates is not included in the calculations. Also, no allowance is made for the distributional effects of inflation and anticipated inflation between creditors and stockholders.

4.7 Conclusion

This chapter has presented some of the aggregate characteristics of a sample of manufacturing firms for the years 1926–27. The results, as regards the postwar period, are broadly consistent with those obtained by other researchers. That is, the data show the increasing importance of external, particularly debt, sources of funds in financing firms' real investment expenditures. The results also illustrate the dramatic decline that has occurred during the past fifteen years in the securities markets' valuation of net assets relative to replacement values, and also relative to rates of return.

Further research will concentrate on using individual firm data to attempt to improve our understanding of the relationships between firm asset and liability structure, and the relationships between firm financing and real investment decisions. A clearer resolution of many of the outstanding issues regarding aggregate relationships between inflation, tax policy, financing and investment decisions, and market valuations requires a better understanding of individual firm behavior.

References

Brainard, William C.; Shoven, J. B.; and Weiss, L. 1980. The Financial Valuation of the Return to Capital. *Brookings Papers on Economic Activity* 2: 453–502.

Feldstein, Martin. 1980. Inflation and the Stock Market. *American Economic Review* 70: 839–47.

Friedman, Benjamin M. 1980. Postwar Changes in American Financial Markets. In Feldstein, Martin, ed., *The American Economy in Transition*. Chicago: University of Chicago Press.

5 Private Pensions as Corporate Debt

Martin Feldstein

Private pensions are now a central feature of the asset and liability structure of the American economy. More than half of all employees have some form of pension coverage. The value to employees of their prospective pension benefits is a major part of their total financial wealth and generally represents the only way in which these individuals hold the debt of American corporations. Indeed, since the great majority of American households have little or no other financial assets, the substitution of future pension benefits for current wages is their only contribution to financing the accumulation of nonresidential capital.[1]

Similarly, the promised pension benefits represent major liabilities of corporations. For many corporations, the present actuarial value of these future benefits constitutes a greater liability than the conventional debts in the form of bonds, commercial paper, and bank loans. By the end of 1981, the aggregate value of just the vested pension liabilities of nonfinancial corporations will probably exceed the corresponding value of all of their other net liabilities.

It is worthwhile, therefore, as part of the NBER general study of the changing character and role of debt and equity in the American economy,

Martin Feldstein is President of the National Bureau of Economic Research and Professor of Economics at Harvard University.

This chapter is in part a summary of two earlier technical studies that were done in the NBER project on the economics of the U.S. pension system and presented in Feldstein (1980) and Feldstein and Seligman (1981). It also draws on Feldstein (1978).

1. In 1972, nearly half of personal tax returns reported no interest and dividend income and more than seventy-five percent reported interest and dividend income of less than five hundred dollars. These figures are quite consistent with survey data that indicate that in that year more than half of the households with a head under the age of sixty-five held no financial assets, and eighty percent held financial assets of less than five thousand dollars. See Feldstein and Feenberg (1981).

to examine the private pension as a form of corporate debt. This chapter begins with an analysis of the ways in which the pension liabilities are and are not like corporate bonds, and then considers some of the conceptual issues involved in valuing future pension benefits. In the second section, I discuss the advantage to firms of fully funding their pension obligations and reasons why many firms nevertheless choose to have unfunded obligations. The third section summarizes the results of research on the effect of unfunded pension liabilities on the equity value of firms.

The first three sections thus consider the role of pensions at the level of the individual firm. In the two sections that follow, I focus on the current and future role of pensions in the national economy. More specifically, section 5.4 examines the effect of private pensions on the nation's saving rate, paying special attention to the implications of unfunded pension obligations. The fifth section then discusses the impact of inflation on the private pension system and the likely future for indexed and unindexed private pensions.

I should emphasize that the ideas presented in this chapter are more in the nature of a progress report than a finished body of research. The final section of the paper comments briefly on a number of questions that remain to be investigated.

5.1   Evaluating Pension Liabilities

The typical pension plan is a corporate promise to pay retirement benefits based on the retiree's number of years of employment and his level of earnings during his immediate preretirement years. Although an employee generally forfeits any claim to benefits if he leaves the company after only a few years of employment, the benefits of an employee who stays with the firm for some minimum number of years become "vested," i.e., the employee becomes entitled to benefits even if he subsequently leaves the company before retirement age. Firms can set aside tax deductible funds to meet these vested future benefit obligations, and the income on these assets is not taxed to either the corporation or the pension plan itself. Some firms fund all of their vested pension obligations, but many do not.

Because the promise to pay future pension benefits is like the promise to pay interest and principal, a pension obligation is similar in many ways to an outstanding corporate bond. This is particularly true when the promised benefit is fixed in nominal terms, as it generally is when an employee is already retired. For an employee who is still working, the level of future pension benefits is not fixed but depends on future earnings. But even for such current employees, the level of *vested* benefits is fixed in nominal terms.

There are, however, a number of significant differences. First, pension obligations are less visible. Unlike corporate bonds, the pension obligations are not recorded on the corporate balance sheet. Present accounting rules require only that firms indicate the extent of their unfunded pension benefits in the notes that accompany the balance sheet. Although this information must be provided in the annual 10–K report that is filed with the Securities and Exchange Commission and that is available to the public, there is no requirement to include any information about pension obligations in the firm's annual report to its shareholders.

Second, pension obligations are more flexible. Although the Employee Retirement Income Security Act (ERISA) rules require firms to follow a policy of funding all new pension obligations within thirty years (and all previous pension obligations in forty years), firms have considerable discretion about timing in the choice of a specific funding plan. Moreover, if a firm experiences temporary financial difficulties, getting permission to delay funding is both easier than postponing debt service and likely to have fewer serious consequences for the firm.

Third, the consequences for the firm of not being able to meet its pension obligations are also limited by government guarantee. If the pension plan or the company becomes bankrupt, the pension obligations become the responsibility of the federally financed Pension Benefits Guarantee Corporation (PBGC) which has recourse to the firm only to the extent of thirty percent of the firm's equity.

The flexibility of timing and the PBGC guarantee reduce the value of the pension obligation relative to a bond with the same potential annual cash outlay. How much the flexibility and guarantee are worth depends upon the circumstances of the particular firm, with a greater effect the less sound the firm's financial position. In the remainder of this section, I shall ignore both of these features, implicitly assuming that the firm's position is so strong that they are irrelevant.

There is a fundamental difference in the tax treatment of bonds and pension obligations that has an important *quantitative* effect on the valuation of pension obligations although it does not imply a *qualitative* difference between bonds and pensions: all the payments made to a pension fund are tax deductible while the principal repayments on a bond are not tax deductible. If the corporation pays a marginal tax rate of fifty percent (including both federal and state taxes), a one-dollar payment of pension benefits by the firm reduces the firm's after-tax profit by only fifty cents. Similarly, a one-dollar contribution to the pension fund to meet *future* benefit obligations also reduces the firm's tax by fifty cents and therefore reduces its after-tax earnings or assets by only fifty cents. In contrast, repaying one dollar of corporate debt involves no tax reduction and therefore reduces assets by a full dollar. It is wrong therefore to regard pension liabilities as equivalent to bonds or loan balances. Indeed, it may be more accurate to treat each dollar of ordinary debt obligations as equal to two dollars of net pension obligations. Equivalently, it is important to measure pension obligations in terms of their net-of-tax cost.[2]

In addition to these differences between pension liabilities and bonds, it is important to recognize that the tax deductibility of pension contributions is logically different from the nontaxability of the earnings of pension fund assets. The fact that these earnings are not taxed has important implications for calculating the present value of future benefit obligations. *In general, the present value of future benefit obligations cannot be calculated by discounting future benefits in the customary way by either the pretax or aftertax rate of interest, but depends on the extent to which (or the speed with which) those benefit obligations are funded.*

An example will clarify why this is so (see Feldstein and Seligman 1981). Consider a firm with an obligation to pay a single pension benefit of one hundred dollars ten years from now. The firm can borrow at an interest rate of twelve percent on its high-quality bonds. Alternatively, it can buy the high-quality (i.e., virtually riskless) bonds of other firms for its pension fund and receive a yield of twelve percent on those bonds. Its combined federal and state marginal tax rate is fifty percent. These figures imply that the net cost of borrowed funds to the firm is six percent, and this is the rate that it should use to calculate the present value of any future pension benefit contributions.[3] However, once a dollar has been contributed, it accumulates at twelve percent inside the pension fund.

Thus, if the firm chooses to fund its future obligation immediately, it need contribute only $32.20 since, at twelve percent, this will accumulate to $100.00 at the end of ten years. Moreover, since the current contribution would be tax deductible, the net cost to the firm would be only $16.10; equivalently, the existence of the $100.00 promised benefit reduces the current equity value of the firm below what it would otherwise be by $16.10. In contrast, if the firm does no funding of the benefit, it must pay $100.00 at the end of ten years. This will have a net-of-tax cost to its shareholders at that time of $50.00. Like other future costs and benefits that are known with (virtual) certainty, this $50.00 can be discounted to a present value of the firm's net interest rate of six percent. The present value calculated in this way is $27.92.

The decision to postpone funding the benefit or to fund it gradually over the ten years implies a present value that depends on both the pretax

2. Note also that a debt repayment reduces gross assets without changing earnings while the payment of a pension obligation reduces both earning and assets according to accounting conventions.

3. This assumes that a small increase in borrowing does not change the interest rate that the firm must pay.

interest rate (twelve percent) and the net-of-tax interest rate (six percent). For example, if the firm decides to wait five years and then to fund fully at that time, it must make a contribution then of $56.74 for a net-of-tax cost of $28.37; i.e., $56.74 accumulates at twelve percent to $100.00 at the end of five years. The present value of the $28.37, discounting at six percent, is $21.20.

Note that, as these calculations suggest, immediate funding is cheaper than any postponement. This implies that firms should in principle fund their obligation as soon as possible. I will return to this subject in the next section.

In practice, a firm typically calculates the present value of the vested pension obligation by discounting the future, actuarially expected, invested pension obligations by an estimate of the yield that it will obtain on its pension portfolio.[4] The value of the unfunded vested pension obligation is then calculated by subtracting the value of its pension assets from this measure of the pension obligation. For the funded portion of the benefits, this is an appropriate comparison; the discount rate is conceptually correct, because there is no need to adjust the funded obligation for its tax deductibility since no further tax deduction will be allowed. But for the unfunded benefits, the usual method of calculation typically *overstates* the true value. To see this, note that the $100.00 promised benefit would conventionally be valued at $32.20 instead of $27.92. Only if the benefit obligation is very far in the future (or growing very rapidly) does the conventional procedure of using a discount rate that is too high more than offset the error of not reflecting the tax deductibility of the contribution or of the direct pension payment by the firm.

In addition to the issues of tax deductibility and of the choice of the discount rate for funded and unfunded obligations, there is the very basic question of whether the obligation should be defined to include only vested benefits or a broader measure of actuarially expected benefits. The narrow focus on vested benefits may understate the true value of a firm's obligation. The accounting requirements focus on the vested benefits because a future benefit does not become a legal liability of the firm until it is vested, i.e., until the employee is entitled to the benefits even if he quits the firm or is fired. The typical plan might provide that an employee with ten years or more of employment has vested benefits of two percent of his final year's earnings per year of service; e.g., a twenty-year employee gets forty percent of his final year's earnings. In this case, the vested pension obligation completely ignores the employee with nine years of service even though he is very likely to stay long enough to become vested. Similarly, the vested benefits of the sixty-four-year-old employee make no allowance for the fact that he is very likely to wait until

---

4. In many cases, this is not even a realistic estimate of the risk-free return but only a conventional assumption designed to be conservative.

he is sixty-five before retiring. The calculation of vested benefits is intentionally myopic. Should it be?

The purpose of evaluating pension liabilities is to assess the firm's future expenses in excess of the value of the services it will receive for those payments. The clearest case to consider is the vested benefits of a retired worker. Since the worker is already retired he will provide no further services; the present actuarial value of his pension rights is a net liability of the firm. Consider next a sixty-four-year-old worker with twenty years of experience who will get forty percent of his final wage if he retires at age sixty-four and forty-two percent if he waits another year. Bulow (1979) has noted, in a very provocative paper, that the employee's opportunity to obtain higher pension benefits by waiting an extra year is irrelevant if the firm and the worker take the extra benefits into account in setting the wage for the extra year of work. More specifically, if the wage for that year is set so that the wage plus the increased value of pension benefits equals the value of the employee's services for that year, there is no excess cost to the firm associated with the employee's postponed retirement. The same argument applies to the individual who has had nine years with the firm and is just about to become vested. If his wage during the tenth year of employment is set so that the sum of the wage and the initial value of the vested pension is equal to the value of the tenth year's services, there is no excess compensation in the prospective benefits.

Although Bulow's (1979) analysis is logically sound, it is not clear how relevant it is in practice. I know of no evidence that wages are adjusted to offset unusually large accruals of benefits. But the relationship between wages and pension benefit accrual is an empirical question that remains to be investigated. Moreover, even if there is not a perfect offset with the implied large jumps in a few particular years, there may be a general tendency for the relationship between earnings and seniority to reflect the accruing pension benefits. If empirical work establishes that there is less than a full-wage offset of the accruing benefits, then the evaluation of pension obligations must go beyond vested benefits in order to give an accurate picture of the firm's net obligation.

5.2 The Pension Funding Puzzle

As I noted in the previous section, the firm can reduce the real net cost of its pension obligations by funding them as fully as possible. This can be shown even more explicitly as follows. Recall that, in the example in the previous section, the firm has a pension benefit of $100.00 to pay in ten years, with a constant twelve percent interest rate on its own debt and on the obligations that it can hold in its pension fund, and has a marginal rate of fifty percent. Funding the benefit immediately would involve the net cost of $16.10.

Assume now that the firm does not wish to fund the future benefits out of its current earnings since it wishes to use those funds for internal investment and dividends. It therefore borrows the $16.10 and uses the borrowed money to fund the future benefit. At the end of one year, it owes interest of twelve percent on the loan of $16.10, or $1.93. Since this interest is a deductible expense, the net cost of the interest is $.97 (or six percent of the loan). Assume that the firm borrows the $.97 and thus increases its loan to $17.07. The loan grows in this way at six percent a year until, at the end of the tenth year, it has grown to $28.83. The firm can repay this loan in the tenth year and use the accumulated pension fund of $50.00 to discharge its pension obligation. In this example, there is no change in the firm's cash flow under either method except in the tenth year, at which time the immediate funding method saves more than forty percent of the cost that would be incurred with no advance funding.

The implications of the example are perfectly general. The firm can borrow at a net-of-tax interest rate and then use the funds to earn a pretax interest rate within the pension fund. Since borrowing and holding debt do not change the total debt position of the firm and pension fund combined, it is essentially an arbitrage opportunity.[5] The puzzle then is why many firms are not fully funded.[6]

Some firms may not fund more rapidly because the tax law limits the speed with which unfunded benefit obligations can be funded with tax deductible contributions. I suspect that this can account for at most a small fraction of the firms, although evidence on this point remains to be collected.

One potential explanation of the apparently irrational behavior of firms is that the management of those firms believes that the securities market is irrational, i.e., that portfolio investors would recognize the additional debt that appears on a firm's balance sheet but not the unfunded pension liability or the asset that it holds in its pension fund. If that were true, it would be in the interest of current shareholders to leave the pension liability unfunded. Although the evidence summarized in the next section indicates that securities investors do not make this mistake, some firms may still be attributing that error to them.

A closely related explanation is that firms may be reluctant to fund more rapidly because the pension contribution would reduce the year's reported earnings (even if financed by borrowing), and this in turn might reduce the firm's market value if securities investors do not understand the reasons for the lower reported earnings. Firms should in principle be

5. There is a separate issue of the type of asset in which the firm should invest its pension fund. Black (1980) and Tepper (1980) have argued that firms should hold only debts in their pension funds since equity investments (if any) are best made on the corporations' own accounts.

6. In a sample of large manufacturing firms, Seligman and I (1981) found that about twenty-five percent of vested benefits were unfunded.

able to avoid this problem by providing such information to shareholders and to the market if it decided to accelerate the funding of pension liabilities.

Firms may be reluctant to borrow in order to finance pension contributions because of the irrational rules of credit-rating organizations, bank regulators, and the like. In an irrational world, it is optimal to behave irrationally—or at least in a way that by logical standards appears to be irrational. Credit ratings, for example, depend on the amount of conventional debt that a firm has, on the ratio of earnings to assumed debt service obligations, and the like. An increase in conventional debt used to finance a pension contribution would appear incorrectly to increase the leverage of the firm, and this might result in a lower-quality rating for the firm's debt obligations. Because certain classes of portfolio investors cannot invest in securities with a low rating, reduction in the credit rating would raise the firm's cost of capital even if informed portfolio investors recognized the error in the lower rating. Similarly bank loan officers may be judged by regulators and by their superiors on the basis of the conventional balance sheet characteristics of the firms to which they make loans. A firm that weakens its conventional balance sheet may lose more through higher costs of borrowing or reduced credit availability than it gained by earlier funding of its pension obligation. Again, we lack evidence on the actual or presumed importance of these effects. Moreover, the entire argument of this paragraph assumes that there are not other investors and lenders who are prepared to arbitrage away such "irrational" credit-rating yield differences. With sufficient arbitrage, the arguments of this paragraph are not valid.

The existence of the Pension Benefits Guarantee Corporation may encourage firms to remain less than fully funded in order to increase the expected value of that compulsory insurance. Since the PBGC guarantees the benefits to the employees, it removes the natural concern of the employees or their unions to keep pensions more fully funded.

Finally, there is the possibility that managers whose salaries or bonuses are based on performance may want to see accounting profits and assets increased even if that means lower real net-of-tax profits to shareholders. Again, such behavior should not be necessary, since the company's board of directors could modify the rules at the suggestion of management to make the interest of shareholders and management coincide.

In short, the pension-funding puzzle—or, more accurately, the non-funding puzzle—remains to be solved.

5.3   Pension Obligations and Share Prices

As part of the NBER Project on the Changing Role of Debt and Equity, Stephanie Seligman and I studied the effect of unfunded pension obligations on the equity value of a sample of manufacturing firms. The analysis used the inflation-adjusted income and assets that large firms have been required to provide for 1976 and subsequent years.

The basic approach of the study was to relate the market value of a firm's equity to the replacement value of its physical assets, its earnings and history of earnings growth, and the value of its debt. The firm's expenditure on research and development and the "beta" coefficient relating movements in the firm's share price to movements of an aggregate share price index were also included in the basic specifications of the statistical valuation equation. By taking these determinants of the market value of the firm into account, we could estimate whether there was an additional statistical effect on the equity value of the unfunded vested pension liabilities reported by the firm.

The evidence for our sample of nearly two hundred manufacturing firms was consistent with the conclusion that share prices fully reflect the value of unfunded pension obligations. Since the conventional accounting measure of the unfunded pension liability has so many problems, it would undoubtedly be more accurate to say that the data are consistent with the conclusion that the securities market appears to accept the conventional measure as the best available information and causes share prices to be reduced by a corresponding amount.

Of course, not all shareholders need be aware of unfunded pension liabilities for this to be true. If a sufficient number of securities analysts and investors representing a significant amount of assets take these liabilities into account, they can make it unnecessary for others to do so.

For nearly two hundred major manufacturing firms in the sample, unfunded pension liabilities averaged 4.9 percent of the replacement value of physical assets in 1977. Since the pension assets themselves averaged 13.5 percent of the replacement value of physical assets, these firms had funded approximately 75.0 percent of their vested pension liabilities. These figures also imply that the value of vested liabilities is extremely large, 18.4 percent of the total value of plant, equipment, and inventory.

It is of course possible that the statistical estimates are spurious. For example, firms that do not fully fund their liabilities may have other characteristics that also depress share values and that were not taken into account in our analysis. For example, firms in very strong financial positions may choose to fund fully while firms with weak earnings may seek to increase reported earnings by not funding as much. The bias could however go in the opposite direction. The firm that expects to have more cash flow in the future may postpone funding. Similarly, the firm with cash that it does not know how to invest may choose to fund more at present. Further analysis of the reasons that firms do not fully fund would help to resolve this statistical issue.

As I noted in the previous section, if the conclusion that the market reflects unfunded liabilities and share prices is correct, this eliminates one reason why firms might wish to be less than fully funded. The evidence that the market recognizes unfunded liabilities also helps to explain why the stock market has not risen more in the past decade. The specific estimates derived from the current sample of firms imply that the unfunded vested pension liabilities were seven percent of the market value of the firm's equity in 1977. If the equity value of the firm was reduced dollar for dollar by its unfunded liability, the recognition of these liabilities lowered the average share value by about seven percent. Stating this in different words, to judge the extent to which shares are currently undervalued, the measure of the "true" equity value of the firm (i.e., the replacement value of physical assets minus net debt) should be reduced by an amount equal to about seven percent of the current market value of equity.

Our investigation of the effect of unfunded pension liabilities on share prices was motivated by the relevance of this issue in assessing the effect of private pensions on the national saving rate. Before commenting on the implications of our findings, I shall discuss the more general issue of the impact of private pensions on national saving (see also Feldstein 1978).

5.4   Private Pensions and National Saving

Although private pensions represent a very substantial amount of capital accumulation, it is not at all clear from a priori considerations alone that they actually achieve any net increase in the nation's capital stock. Private pensions may represent a change in only the form in which individuals save, a substitution of pension assets for an equal amount of direct saving. Indeed, since the untaxed pension fund earns a higher rate of return than the taxpaying individual, the pension permits the same level of retirement consumption to be financed with a smaller initial volume of savings.

The existence of private pension plans increases aggregate national saving only if it induces individuals to postpone consumption, i.e., to consume more in retirement and less when they are working.[7] Pensions may of course induce such a shift in consumption in response to the higher rate of return. If the increase in retirement consumption is large enough,

---

7. This statement implicitly assumes that the existence of the private pension does not alter the total amount of government spending in each year. The private pension plan per se involves a postponement of tax liability from the earning years to the retirement years. This in itself increases private savings. But the lower tax payments imply an equal decrease in government saving or increase in government borrowing. This change in the timing of tax payments therefore leaves national saving unchanged.

saving will rise. While this condition will not be satisfied for all taxpayers, it will be for some.

In addition to those who increase their desired saving, there is another important group for whom the private pension represents *forced* saving. The very substantial fraction of the population with little or no directly held financial wealth implies that forced saving may be quite important. These individuals may be myopic or may believe that their Social Security benefits will provide at least as much as they want for retirement. In any case, they are forced by their private pensions to have more retirement consumption than they would otherwise choose. Although they might in principle offset this extra pension wealth by borrowing, it is extremely difficult to borrow any substantial amount without specific collateral. Whether it is this difficulty or just an aversion to the accumulation of debt, few individuals reach retirement with enough financial liabilities to offset a significant fraction of their pension benefits.

Pensions may also increase saving by inducing individuals to retire earlier than they otherwise would. Since pensions are paid only when an individual retires, individuals have a strong financial incentive to retire as soon as they are eligible for the maximum pension. When an individual retires at an earlier age, he has more years of consumption to finance and fewer years in which to accumulate the retirement assets. Induced early retirement would therefore increase saving even among individuals who do not respond at all to the higher rate of return.

Although the empirical evidence on this issue is weak, it seems likely on the basis of existing data that the promise of private pension benefits does not induce an equal or greater reduction in direct personal saving. But, even if direct personal saving falls by less than the amount required to fund the private pension, total private saving may fall if the pension is in fact not funded. I say "may" rather than "will" because, even with no funding, total saving may increase. What happens depends crucially on the response of shareholders.

To understand this, consider the case in which the firm trades a promise of a future pension benefit for a reduction in current wages below what they would otherwise be. Assume that the employees recognize the value of the promised pension and reduce their saving by enough to keep retirement consumption unchanged. If the firm uses the extra profits that result from the lower wages to fund the pension, there is just a substitution of one form of saving for another.[8]

But what if the firm does not fund the pension liability and instead adds the extra profits to retirement earnings and invests them in the firm. This

---

8. This ignores the differences in tax treatment between pensions and direct saving, a simplification that greatly facilitates discussing the current point without losing anything essential.

too is just a substitution of one form of saving for another unless the shareholders respond to the increased earnings and assets by consuming more. This increase in consumption would occur if the firm's share price rose in response to the increased plant and equipment, i.e., if the shareholders ignored the increased pension liability in valuing their shares. The evidence (presented in the previous section) that share prices do reflect the unfunded pension liability implies that shareholders would not be misled by the increase in assets. Instead, the change in corporate assets and the change in pension liability would offset each other and leave the share price and therefore shareholder consumption unchanged.

A similar argument applies if the firm uses the extra profits to finance higher dividends. Since the higher dividend does not reflect higher real earnings or greater assets, the share price would remain unchanged, and shareholders should not increase their consumption in response to the higher level of dividends. Unlike the analysis of retained earnings, this argument requires both that the share price not rise and that shareholders base their consumption on the value of their wealth and not on dividends per se. Since some macroeconomic evidence does suggest that dividends are important as a determinant of consumption, unfunded pension liabilities may induce some additional consumption on the part of shareholders.

The effect on the nation's savings of an increase in private pensions is thus quite complex. It seems likely that there is some increase in retirement consumption and that employees do not reduce their direct savings by the present value of the pension obligation. To the extent that these obligations are funded or used to increase retained earnings, aggregate savings increase. To the extent that the extra cash flow that results from unfunded benefits goes into dividends, the net effect is more ambiguous.

To conclude this discussion, it is worthwhile to emphasize the difference between unfunded private pension benefits and unfunded Social Security benefits. Because the promise of future pension benefits is an obligation of corporate shareholders, it is reflected in a market price that reduces the net wealth of current shareholders. Because the promise of private pension benefits makes current shareholders poorer, they have an incentive to save more either directly or through corporate retained earnings. The same is not true for Social Security. The promise to pay future benefits implies a higher tax on future employees but involves no incentive for current employees to save more.[9] Thus, whatever the depressing effect of either type of pension on the direct savings of employees, private pensions will result in a larger increase in national savings (or smaller decrease) than would result from an equal amount of Social Security.

9. This ignores the observation of Barro (1974) that current individuals may wish to save more in order to increase their bequest to compensate their children for the higher taxes that those children will face as a result of increased Social Security benefits.

5.5   Private Pensions and Inflation

Much of the recent discussion about the relation between private pensions and inflation has emphasized the adverse impact that the unexpected rise in inflation during the past fifteen years has had on pension recipients and on the performance of pension funds. Some of those who have commented on the problem have even concluded that the private pension system cannot survive in an inflationary economy. It is important, however, not to confuse the unfortunate consequences that followed when inflation caught pensioners and pension fund managers by surprise with the inability to adjust to future conditions, even uncertain future conditions.

In a previous study (Feldstein 1981a), I concluded that a steady rate of inflation, far from destroying the pension system, would actually increase the share of total savings that goes into private pensions. The reason for this conclusion is that the advantage that the private pension has in exempting its portfolio income from taxation becomes greater when there is inflation. This in turn reflects the fact that individuals pay tax on the full nominal interest income that they earn on direct saving and therefore pay a tax per unit of capital that rises with the rate of inflation; in contrast, of course, since pensions pay no tax on their interest income, the tax differential per unit of capital rises with inflation. Similarly, individuals pay tax on nominal capital gains on stock (as well as on dividends), and this capital gains tax also implies a tax per unit of capital that rises with the rate of inflation. Thus, on both debt and equity, inflation increases the yield differential between household and pension funds in favor of pensions.

The *relative* yields on debt and equity are likely to move in opposite directions for households and pensions. If the real pretax interest rate remains unchanged, the pensions have a constant real yield on debt while the yield on equity falls slightly because of the extra taxes paid at the corporate level. For households, the real net-of-tax yield on debt falls sharply while the real yield on equity falls by less. Households would thus be induced to sell debt to pension funds and hold more equity directly.

The uncertainty of inflation influences the optimal extent of pension indexing and the likely composition of pension assets. Without indexing, the vested pension obligations are nominal long-term liabilities of the firm. The firm can hedge these liabilities by holding long-term bonds. Of course, firms may nevertheless invest in equities because they believe that the equity yield is high enough to compensate for the reduced hedging. But, since the extra risk of equity investment is borne by the firm's shareholders, the employees who participate in the pension plan should earn an implicit nominal return on their foregone wages that is equal to only the nominal return on riskless bonds.

A fully indexed pension would make all pension obligations real. Long-term bonds are clearly an inappropriate investment for funding such real obligations. Stocks can provide a hedge against price level uncertainties only by accepting substantial general uncertainty. Bodie (1980) has emphasized that a portfolio with a minimum-variance real return would be invested almost completely in short-term debt (with a small amount in commodity futures) and that the expected return on such a portfolio is approximately zero. If employees are so risk averse that they choose a fully indexed pension, the implicit real return that they earn on foregone wages should therefore also be approximately zero. Again, firms may invest in equities, but the shareholders rather than the pensioners should receive any extra yield in return for bearing that risk.

If employees choose a partially indexed position, i.e., one in which benefits rise less than one-for-one with the price level or in which benefits depend on the return on the pension fund assets, the firm can invest in a way that permits giving a higher return to pension participants while compensating shareholders for any additional risk that they bear. The optimal extent of pension indexing depends on the risk aversion of employees and the cost, in terms of the reduction in the expected yield, of investing pension assets to produce a constant real return.

As Samuelson (1958) noted years ago, an unfunded social security program can provide an annuity with an implicit real rate of return equal to the real growth rate of the economy, probably about three percent a year over the next decade or longer. Although three percent is substantially less than the real return of more than ten percent that the nation as a whole earns on additions to the stock of plant and equipment (Feldstein and Poterba 1980), the political pressure to substitute unfunded Social Security benefits for private pensions (or vice versa) is likely to depend on the real *after-tax* yield that partly indexed pensions can offer and on the associated risk. If employees were completely risk averse, the low three percent yield on Social Security would look good in comparison to Bodie's zero yield on a minimum-variance real return portfolio. But if employees are willing to accept the risk inherent in a partially indexed pension, they can expect to receive an implicit yield that is much greater than three percent.

In summary, the form and funding of private pensions will probably change in the coming decade if inflation continues at recent levels but, unless employees become much more risk averse, private pensions are likely to continue to finance a growing share of retirement consumption.[10]

5.6   Future Research

The substantial size and rapid growth of private pensions make it important to understand their impact on capital markets and capital

---

10. This section summarizes conclusions developed in Feldstein (1980 and 1981b).

formation. From the basic problem of pension liability measurement to the more complex issue of the impact of unfunded obligations on shareholder consumption, we are only beginning to do the necessary research. This chapter has indicated a number of questions on which further research should be done. How do employees' earnings reflect their accruing pension benefits? Why do firms not take advantage of the tax benefits of full and immediate funding? How do financial markets and financial institutions respond to the extent of a company's pension fund? And how does the existence of partly funded private pensions influence the nation's aggregate rate of saving? As the answers to these questions become known, we will better understand the impact of private pensions on the American economy.

References

Barro, Robert. 1974. Are Government Bonds Net Wealth? *Journal of Political Economy* 82: 1095–1117.

Black, Fisher. 1980. The Tax Advantages of Pension Fund Investments in Bonds. NBER Working Paper No. 533. August.

Bodie, Zvi. 1980. Purchasing Power Annuities: Financial Innovation for Stable Real Retirement Income in an Inflationary Environment. NBER Working Paper No. 442. February.

Bulow, Jeremy. 1979. Analysis of Pension Funding under ERISA. NBER Working Paper No. 402. November.

Feldstein, Martin. 1978. Do Private Pensions Increase National Savings? *Journal of Public Economics* 10: 277–293.

Feldstein, Martin. 1981a. Private Pensions and Inflation. *American Economic Review*, 71 (2): 424–428.

Feldstein, Martin 1981b. "Should Private Pensions be Indexed?" NBER Working Paper No. 787. October.

Feldstein, Martin, and Feenberg, Daniel. 1981. Alternative Tax Rules and Personal Savings Incentives: Microeconomic Data and Behavioral Simulations. In M. Feldstein, ed., *Behavioral Simulation in Tax Policy Analysis*, NBER conference volume, forthcoming.

Feldstein, Martin, and Poterba, James. 1980. State and Local Taxes and the Rate of Return on Nonfinancial Corporate Capital. NBER Working Paper No. 508R. July.

Feldstein, Martin, and Seligman, Stephanie. 1981. Pension Funding, Share Prices and National Saving. *Journal of Finance* 36 (4): 801–824.

Samuelson, Paul. 1958. An Exact Consumption-Loan Model of Interest with or without the Social Contrivance of Money. *Journal of Political Economy* 66: 467–82.

Tepper, Irwin. 1980. Taxation and Corporate Pension Policy. Mimeographed.

6 Debt and Economic Activity in the United States

Benjamin M. Friedman

Businesses and individuals, in an economy like that of the United States, can finance their activities in a rich variety of ways. Businesses investing in new plant and equipment can rely on internally generated funds, or they can raise external funds from the financial markets. When they do turn to external sources of funds, they can issue either debt obligations or new equity shares in the enterprise. Individuals can likewise use their own or borrowed funds to make major purchases like automobiles, and many individuals can also borrow to finance ordinary consumer spending as well as major hard goods. Even in arranging home purchases, transactions that are almost always partly debt financed, individuals usually can choose what fraction of the purchase price initially represents their own equity. In principle, businesses and individuals are continually making these and other financing choices on the basis of yield comparisons, credit availability, and other considerations, so that the total amount of debt financing does not necessarily have to bear any close relationship to the underlying economic activity.

In fact, however, the relationship between outstanding debt and economic activity in the United States is remarkably steady—indeed, just as steady as the more widely recognized and better understood relationship between economic activity and money. The aggregate outstanding indebtedness of all nonfinancial borrowers in the United States has been approximately $1.40 for each $1.00 of the economy's gross national

Benjamin M. Friedman is Professor of Economics at Harvard University and Program Director for Financial Markets and Monetary Economics at the National Bureau of Economic Research.

This chapter draws in large part on the author's earlier research, especially Friedman (1981). The author gratefully acknowledges research support from the National Bureau, the National Science Foundation, and the Alfred P. Sloan Foundation.

product, ever since World War II. Throughout the postwar period the overall debt-to-income ratio has displayed neither trend nor cyclical variation.

Moreover, the stability of the U.S. economy's outstanding debt in relation to its income has not merely represented the stability of a sum of stable parts, as is apparently the case (apart from trend) among the familiar monetary aggregates. Neither private sector debt nor government debt has borne a stable relationship to economic activity, but their total has. In particular, the secular rise and procyclical fluctuation in the private sector's debt have approximately offset the corresponding secular decline (relative to income) and countercyclical fluctuation in the federal government's debt.

The stability of the debt-to-income relationship, if it is indeed a regularity that will persist, bears a number of important implications for the U.S. economy. The finding that debt is as reliably related to economic activity as is money has immediate implications for the choice of monetary policy target. It is also potentially relevant for fiscal policy, in that some hypotheses that may explain the observed debt-to-income stability bear strong implications for the "crowding out" of private investment by debt-financed government spending. Finally, it is especially important in the context of the current widespread concern over capital formation in the U.S. economy. The financing of an increased capital formation rate in the 1980s, as well as the aggregate-level risk to the economy associated with that financing, depends in large part on issues underlying the debt-to-income relationship.

The object of this chapter is to examine the debt-to-income stability phenomenon in the United States, with particular attention to implications for the financing of capital formation. Section 6.1 explains in what sense the economy's outstanding debt is stable in relation to its income. Section 6.2 reports on some empirical comparisons of relative stability for different liability and asset aggregates. Section 6.3 outlines three separate hypotheses that could plausibly account for the observed debt-to-income stability, emphasizing the economic implications of these hypotheses, and briefly reports on some preliminary attempts to test them empirically. To anticipate, findings thus far along these lines are largely inconclusive, so that the debt-to-income stability phenomenon itself, while well documented, remains something of a puzzle. Section 6.4 concludes the chapter by briefly considering some implications of debt-to-income stability for the financing of U.S. capital formation.

6.1   Debt and Income in the Postwar Period

Table 6.1 presents data showing the year-end indebtedness of U.S nonfinancial borrowers, as a percentage of fourth-quarter gross national product, for each year since 1945. The first column of the table shows the total credit market indebtedness of all U.S. nonfinancial borrowers. The next five columns present comparable data dividing this total into the respective indebtedness of each of five specific borrowing sectors. The table's final column shows, as a memorandum item, comparable data (not included in the total in the first column) for the debt issued in U.S. markets by foreign borrowers.[1] Figure 6.1 plots the total nonfinancial debt ratio and its five components by sector.

These data are "net" in the sense that they net out financial intermediation. In other words, the data include such items as a household's mortgage issued to a bank, or a corporation's bonds sold to an insurance company, but they exclude any liability issued in turn by the bank or the insurance company in order to finance that lending activity. The data also exclude debt issued by separate financial subsidiaries of nonfinancial corporations, as well as by federally sponsored credit agencies and mortgage pools. The data are "gross," however, in the sense that they include all of an individual household or firm's outstanding credit market liabilities, not just any excess of liabilities over either financial or total assets, and also in the sense that they include one household's borrowing from another or one firm's borrowing from another.

The strong stability of the total nonfinancial debt ratio, shown in the top line in Figure 6.1 and the first column of Table 6.1, stands out in stark contrast to the variation of the individual sector components. The nonfinancial economy's reliance on debt, scaled in relation to economic activity, has shown almost no trend and but little variation since World War II. During this period the total nonfinancial debt ratio has trended slightly upward, apart from a dip in the first few postwar years, and has also exhibited a slight cyclicality, typically rising a point or two in recession years (when gross national product, in the denominator, is weak).

The individual components of this total, however, have varied in sharply different directions both secularly and cyclically. In brief, the secular postwar rise in private debt has largely mirrored a substantial decline (relative to economic activity) in federal government debt, while cyclical bulges in federal debt issuance have mostly had their counterpart in the abatement of private borrowing. Households have almost continuously increased their reliance on debt in relation to their nonfinancial activity throughout this period. Both corporations and unincorporated businesses have also issued steadily more debt, on a relative basis, except for temporary retrenchments during recession years. State and local governments steadily increased their relative debt-issuing activity during the 1950s and '60s, but just as steadily reduced it during the 1970s. Except only for 1975–76 and 1980, the federal government has reduced its debt

---

1. In part because of the capital export controls that were in force during 1964–74, foreign obligors accounted for only a small fraction of borrowing in the U.S. markets throughout this period.

Table 6.1   Outstanding Debt of U.S. Nonfinancial Borrowers

	Total	Federal Government	State and Local Governments	Business Corporations	Other Businesses	Households	Memorandum: Foreign
1946	155.6%	103.4%	7.0%	22.4%	7.0%	16.0%	3.6%
1947	145.5	90.5	6.9	23.3	7.0	18.0	5.0
1948	138.2	80.9	7.2	23.7	7.0	19.6	5.2
1949	149.3	84.8	8.4	25.2	7.6	23.5	5.4
1950	133.1	70.7	8.2	23.3	7.4	23.7	4.6
1951	126.6	63.7	8.1	23.5	7.4	24.1	4.3
1952	127.8	61.5	8.7	24.1	7.5	26.0	4.2
1953	134.5	62.9	9.7	25.1	7.5	29.3	4.5
1954	136.8	61.4	11.0	25.5	7.7	31.2	4.4
1955	133.8	56.0	11.3	25.4	7.8	33.3	4.0
1956	133.4	51.9	11.6	26.5	7.9	35.5	4.0
1957	135.8	50.0	12.3	28.0	8.2	37.4	4.2
1958	137.2	49.5	12.9	28.5	8.3	38.1	4.5
1959	140.9	48.2	13.5	28.9	8.7	40.6	4.3
1960	143.9	46.8	14.3	30.5	9.1	43.3	4.6

Year							
1961	141.9	44.8	14.2	30.3	9.2	43.3	4.7
1962	143.2	43.6	14.4	30.8	9.6	44.8	4.9
1963	143.5	41.6	14.6	30.9	10.2	46.3	5.1
1964	145.3	40.2	14.7	31.3	10.9	48.3	5.5
1965	141.0	36.6	14.3	31.1	11.0	47.9	5.3
1966	139.1	34.4	14.1	32.0	11.4	47.4	5.1
1967	140.3	33.9	14.2	33.4	11.6	47.2	5.3
1968	139.0	32.5	14.1	34.0	11.5	46.8	5.1
1969	140.2	30.0	14.4	35.5	11.9	47.4	5.1
1970	141.8	29.8	14.8	37.3	12.2	47.7	5.1
1971	141.9	29.4	15.1	37.0	12.6	47.7	5.0
1972	140.3	27.6	14.7	37.0	13.0	47.9	4.9
1973	139.5	25.4	14.1	37.9	13.3	48.8	4.9
1974	141.9	24.4	14.2	40.7	13.5	49.1	5.5
1975	140.6	27.5	13.8	38.8	12.9	47.6	5.9
1976	142.2	29.1	13.4	38.3	12.7	48.7	6.5
1977	143.0	28.8	13.0	38.0	12.7	50.5	6.5
1978	141.0	27.6	12.4	37.2	12.5	51.3	7.3
1979	143.1	26.6	11.9	38.3	13.1	53.3	7.4
1980	142.8	27.2	11.8	38.4	13.1	52.4	7.8

Data are year-end credit market debt totals as percentages of fourth-quarter gross national product, seasonally adjusted, at annual rate.
Detail may not add to totals because of rounding.
SOURCE: Board of Governors of the Federal Reserve System.

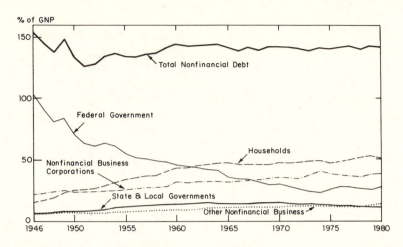

Fig. 6.1   Outstanding Debt of U.S. Nonfinancial Borrowers, 1946–80.

ratio in every year since 1953, although this relative debt reduction has been slower in years when recession has temporarily inflated its deficit (and, again, depressed gross national product in the denominator).

Although the principal focus of this chapter is on the postwar experience shown in Table 6.1 and Figure 6.1, it is also useful to consider briefly the history of the economy's debt ratio in a longer time frame. Figure 6.2 shows the size and composition of the U.S. nonfinancial debt ratio (with corporations and unincorporated businesses aggregated) for 1918–78. Apart from a one-time adjustment associated with the fall of prices after World War I, the U.S. nonfinancial economy's reliance on debt relative to economic activity showed essentially no trend over these sixty years.

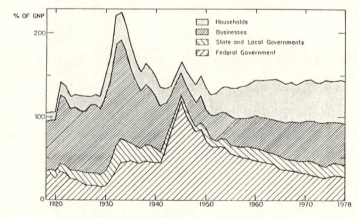

Fig. 6.2   Outstanding Debt of U.S. Nonfinancial Borrowers, 1918–78.
                    From Friedman (1980).

At 143 percent as of year-end 1978, the debt ratio was virtually unchanged from 142 percent in 1921. Nonfinancial borrowers' outstanding debt rose significantly in relation to gross national product only during the Depression years 1930–33, when gross national product itself not only was well below trend but also was falling too rapidly for the pay-down of debt to keep pace.[2] Otherwise the economy's total nonfinancial debt ratio remained roughly steady throughout this period, and the postwar stability therefore appears to be in large part a continuation of a pattern that dates back at least to the 1920s.

6.2 Comparative Stability Analysis

In order to determine that a relationship is stable, it is important to have at hand some benchmark for comparative purposes. In other words, if the debt-to-income relationship is to be judged "stable," then stable in comparison with what? Table 6.2 indicates five liability aggregates (including total nonfinancial debt, as shown in ratio form in Table 6.1 and Figure 6.1) and five asset aggregates used for such comparative purposes in a series of tests of the stability of each of these aggregates in relation to U.S. economic activity during 1953–78.[3] In brief, the results of these tests, drawn from Friedman 1981, are as follows:

Comparison of Ratios. Table 6.1 shows the ratio of the U.S. economy's total nonfinancial debt to gross national product. One form of relative stability test is simply to compare the variability of this ratio over time, as measured by its coefficient of variation (standard deviation divided by the mean), with that of analogous ratios for other liability or asset aggregates. As the first and third columns of Table 6.3 show, this comparison for data including time trends indicates that total net assets and total nonfinancial debt are (in that order) the most stable, while the M1 money stock and the monetary base (in that order) are the least stable, among the ten aggregates. The corresponding comparison for detrended data, shown in the adjacent columns of Table 6.3, again indicates that total net assets is the most stable aggregate in relation to gross national product, with total debt and total nonfinancial debt, respectively, a close second and third. The monetary base exhibits the least stability on a detrended basis, with private nonfinancial liabilities and the M1 money stock close behind. Orderings based on annual data are essentially the same as those based on quarterly data.

2. The debt ratio peak during 1918–78 occurred in 1933, the trough year of the Depression. In addition, much of the household and business debt nominally outstanding during the Depression was of questionable value.

3. It is important to exclude the earlier data because of the behavior of the monetary aggregates while the Federal Reserve System stabilized government bond prices before the Treasury–Federal Reserve Accord.

Table 6.2   Liability and Asset Aggregates Used for Relative Stability Tests

Liability Aggregates	Definition
Total nonfinancial debt	Total credit market liabilities of all U.S. nonfinancial sectors.
Nonfederal debt	Total nonfinancial debt *less* credit market liabilities of the federal government.
Private nonfinancial debt	Nonfederal debt *less* credit market liabilities of state and local governments.
Total debt	Total nonfinancial debt *plus* credit market debt of U.S. financial intermediaries.
Bank credit	Commercial bank loans and investments.

Asset Aggregates	Definition
Monetary base	Bank reserves *plus* currency outside banks.
Money (M1)	Currency outside banks *plus* demand deposits.
Money (M2)	Money (M1) *plus* savings and small time deposits at commercial banks.
Money (M3)	Money (M2) *plus* savings and small time deposits at thrift institutions.
Total net assets	Total holdings of credit market instruments by U.S. nonfinancial holders.

Table 6.3   Results of Comparative Stability Tests

| | Coefficient of Variation, 1953–78 | | | | Regression Standard Error | |
| | Annual Data | | Quarterly Data | | Quarterly Data | |
	Raw	Detrended	Raw	Detrended	1953–78	1970–78
Liability Aggregates						
Total nonfinancial debt	2.5%	1.8%	2.0%	1.9%	.91%	.90%
Nonfederal debt	11.9	4.1	12.3	4.1	.92	.89
Private nonfinancial debt	12.4	3.5	12.6	3.5	.90	.91
Total debt	5.2	1.6	5.4	1.8	.89	.83
Bank credit	6.8	3.2	6.8	3.2	.97	.91
Asset Aggregates						
Monetary base	16.5%	5.1%	16.8%	5.2%	.95%	.99%
Money (M1)	22.3	3.6	22.0	3.6	.88	.90
Money (M2)	4.3	2.9	4.4	2.8	.91	.96
Money (M3)	3.4[a]	1.9[a]	3.5[a]	1.8[a]	.77[a]	.95
Total net assets	1.5	1.4	1.6	1.5	.85	.84

[a]Based on data for 1960–78.

Nominal Income Regressions. Simple ratios of precisely contemporaneous observations may well fail to capture the relevant concept of "stability" in the relationship among variables that move over time with some general lead or lag pattern between them. A second relative stability test therefore involves estimating ten regression equations, in each case relating the growth of nominal gross national product to a moving average of the growth of one of the ten financial aggregates listed in Table 6.2, plus a moving average of a fiscal policy measure, along the lines made familiar by the Federal Reserve Bank of St. Louis. As the fifth column of Table 6.3 shows, total net assets performs best in this test based on quarterly data for 1953–78, with a standard error of 0.85 percent per quarter in "explaining" the historical growth of gross national product, while bank credit (standard error 0.97 percent) performs worst.[4] Total nonfinancial debt is about in the middle. Because the evidence indicates at least some significant break in each of the underlying regressions at around 1970, the last column of Table 6.3 also shows the respective standard errors for analogous regression equations based on data for 1970–78 only. For this shorter period the relative performance of total nonfinancial debt is somewhat better, equaling that of the M1 money stock.

Richer Dynamic Representations. In part because of the extent to which regressions of the St. Louis form have been discredited by a variety of criticisms, researchers examining the money-to-income (or, here, debt-to-income) relationship have increasingly turned to methods that allow for a richer dynamic interaction between money and income by relating the variation of income not to the entirety of the variation of money but only to that part of it which cannot already be deduced either from the past history of money itself or from the joint past history of both money and income.[5] In this context a key indication of the stability of the relationship to income of any financial aggregate is the behavior of that relationship following just such an "innovation," or unanticipated movement, in the aggregate. The aggregate-to-income ratio, of course, rises at first after a positive innovation, but it will then fall back toward a normal position if the rise in the aggregate induces a subsequent rise in income (or a reversal in the aggregate itself). Both the timing and the magnitude of the ratio's return to normal provide important information about the stability of the dynamic aggregate-to-income relationship.

4. An equation with standard error of 0.85 percent would be expected to predict the GNP growth rate to within ±0.85 percent two-thirds of the time. This ranking ignores the superior result for M3 based on a shorter sample period.

5. Among the most important criticisms of the St. Louis approach have been those of Goldfeld and Blinder (1972), Sargent (1976), and Modigliani and Ando (1976). The methodology underlying the tests described below is due largely to Granger and Sims; see especially Sims (1980).

Experimentation along these lines indicates that, on the whole, there is little ground for distinguishing the stability of any one of the five *asset* aggregates listed in Table 6.2 from that of any other. The same is not true for the five *liability* aggregates, however. Here only the total nonfinancial debt ratio (again, the series shown in Table 6.1), and to a lesser extent the bank credit ratio, return to their initial values rapidly and without overshooting after a shock to the relevant aggregate. What is especially interesting in these results is the contrast between the performance of the ratio for total nonfinancial debt and the ratios for nonfederal debt and private debt (both of which are just components of the total) as well as the broader total debt measure. Both the private debt ratio and the nonfederal debt ratio continue to move farther away from their initial values for two years in response to an innovation in the relevant aggregate, and neither shows any significant return to its initial value within five years— hardly a demonstration of stability. Once federal government debt is included, however, the total nonfinancial debt ratio exhibits just as much stability in this context as does any of the five asset ratios. Moreover, proceeding to broaden the liability aggregate further by including financial intermediaries' credit market liabilities results only in lessened apparent stability.

Among the various liability measures considered, therefore, these results suggest that there is indeed something unique about total nonfinancial debt. It is as if the M1 money stock ratio were sharply unstable, but adding commercial bank time and saving deposits to form the M2 money stock ratio yielded stability, and further adding thrift institution deposits to form the M3 money stock ratio destroyed that stability—none of which appears to happen. Hence not only does the total nonfinancial debt ratio exhibit just as much stability as any of the five asset ratios in these dynamic tests, but it does so uniquely among the various liability aggregates tested.[6]

Overview.   In sum, the evidence provided by these three different kinds of tests shows that at least one aggregate measure of outstanding debt liabilities—total nonfinancial debt—consistently exhibits just as much stability in relation to economic activity as do the more familiar asset aggregates including the money stock (however measured). Indeed, some of these tests suggest that the debt-to-income relationship, measured in this way, is more stable than any of the various money-to-income relationships. Regardless of whether the U.S. debt-to-income relationship is "as stable as" or "more stable than" that for money, however, like the money-to-income relationship it is potentially important for understanding the economy. By contrast, although the money-to-income

---

6. Similar tests that distinguish between effects on real income and effects on prices in the reaction of nominal income (not described in the text) show essentially identical results.

relationship has long been the focus of attention, the debt-to-income relationship has to date received little notice.

6.3   Three Possible Explanations

What accounts for this stability? Well-accepted models of the role of money in the economic process suggest a close relationship to income on a priori grounds, but what little study the role of debt has received in the literature thus far has not appeared to indicate any necessarily close or stable relationship to income. Explaining the observed stability of the debt-to-income relationship therefore presents a major research challenge.

A useful starting place for thinking about the underlying economic behavior that could plausibly explain the observed stability of the relationship between the nonfinancial economy's total liabilities and its income is the familiar proposition that, because people hold wealth for the stream of services (positive for assets, negative for liabilities) it provides, they therefore maintain some approximately fixed target for overall wealth in relation to their incomes. Each person's wealth-to-income target is age specific, of course, but if the age structure of the population is roughly stable over time the economy's aggregate wealth-to-income ratio will be approximately stable as well.[7]

Work to date suggests three potential explanations for a stable debt-to-income ratio, each of which proceeds from the assumption of a stable wealth-to-income ratio for the economy as a whole.

An Ultrarationality Hypothesis.   One such potential explanation is an "ultrarationality" hypothesis that in part recasts into stock-flow form work by David and Scadding (1974) intended to explain the stability of the U.S. gross private saving rate as noted earlier by Denison (1958). If the streams of services (again, positive for assets and negative for liabilities) provided by specific components of overall wealth are imperfect substitutes for one another, then the same analysis that implies a stable target wealth in relation to income also implies a stable "subtarget" for each component—including indebtedness. If, in addition, individuals "see through the shell" of government and corporations, as David and Scadding (1974) argued, then they will regard debt obligations issued by the government (for the case of taxpayers) and by corporations (for shareholders) as equivalent to their own liabilities.

Under the ultrarationality hypothesis, therefore, the observed stability of the aggregate debt-to-income relationship has primarily reflected the response of the private sector to movements in the government's indebt-

7. Modigliani (1966) provided a clear discussion of these propositions, showing how they are derivable from more fundamental principles.

edness. Given any variation in the government's liabilities, for whatever purposes may be indicated by public policy, the private sector consisting of households and the corporations that the households own will simply adjust by issuing enough debt to offset the government's action. Yet a further elaboration of the same basic idea that changes nothing fundamental is to view corporations as also responding to independent objectives or influences (for example, tax laws), and households as then adjusting their debt positions to offset the given actions of both the government and the corporations. In either case, the nonfinancial economy will seek (and achieve) a stable ratio of its aggregate liabilities to income, regardless of the composition of that aggregate.

The ultrarationality hypothesis is interesting for several reasons that go beyond its potential ability to explain the debt-to-income stability phenomenon. From a purely behavioral standpoint it carries strong implications about individuals' perceptions and about familiar aspects of wealth holding. In addition, as David and Scadding (1974) have pointed out, it implies that people regard as close substitutes personal saving and corporate saving, as well as personal consumption and taxes. Hence "crowding out ex ante" renders fiscal policy impotent in both the short and the long run.

A Capital-Leveraging Hypothesis.   A second potential explanation is a "capital-leveraging" hypothesis that emphasizes credit market imperfections and the need of most would-be borrowers to provide some kind of collateral, explicit or implicit, in order to obtain credit. To the extent that people do not see through the shell of government, or that the distribution of tax liabilities and the distribution of bond holdings overlap only weakly, the private sector's assets (after netting out inside debt) consist of tangible assets—including not only corporate assets like plant and equipment but also residential real estate and consumer durables—plus government bonds. If people have not only a stable target for net wealth but also a stable subtarget for total assets in relation to income, then they will vary their holdings of tangible assets so as to offset variations in the government's outstanding indebtedness. Variations in the private sector's holdings of tangible assets also typically affect its borrowing capacity, however. When collateral constraints are binding, the increase in tangible asset holdings that follows as a consequence of a reduction in the government's indebtedness therefore facilitates a corresponding increase in the private sector's outstanding liabilities.

The importance of credit market constraints is most readily apparent in the household sector's debt arrangements. In fact, borrowing against tangible assets in the form of home mortgage and consumer installment credit has constituted the overwhelming majority of the household sector's credit market indebtedness at least since World War II (89 percent as of year-end 1980). Similarly, the borrowing of many corporations consists primarily of explicitly secured long-term market debt, in the form of mortgages or "first-mortgage" bonds, and implicitly secured short-term bank debt matched by inventory holdings.

If credit market collateral constraints restrict the private sector's ability to substitute its own liabilities in place of the government's declining indebtedness, the private sector can increase its outstanding liabilities only to the extent that it is also accumulating more tangible assets with which to back them. Under the capital-leveraging hypothesis, therefore, the stability of the U.S. nonfinancial debt ratio has reflected in the first instance an increase in tangible assets in approximately the proportion necessary to hold the private sector's net worth fixed in relation to income, as its ownership of government liabilities has declined relative to income. By easing the effective credit market constraints, this relative increase in tangible assets facilitates the increase in private sector liabilities. If private liabilities increase fully in step with tangible asset holdings, while tangible assets increase in step with the reduction in government debt, then total nonfinancial debt (private plus government) will remain stable in relation to income.

The capital-leveraging hypothesis also bears a number of potentially interesting implications apart from any connection to the stable debt-to-income relationship. Probably the most important of these is the picture it provides of the importance of collateral constraints in the everyday working of the credit markets. In addition, it implies that the government's deficit is a major determinant of the economy's physical investment. Unlike the ultrarationality hypothesis, however, it implies no necessary connection between consumption and taxes, so that fiscal policy can affect not just the composition of income but also its total.

An Asset Demand Hypothesis. Finally—at least with respect to work done thus far—a third potential explanation is that the appearance of stability in the economy's liability-issuing behavior is merely a consequence of balance sheet identities and market-clearing conditions imposed on stable asset-holding behavior. If the separate streams of services provided by tangible assets and financial assets are imperfect substitutes, then people will have stable subtargets in relation to income for the two asset classes separately. In other words, the demand for financial assets, given income, will be relatively interest inelastic. Since total financial assets held must equal total financial assets issued, however, the combination of inelastic demand and an at least partly elastic supply will also result in a stable relationship between income and total financial assets issued.[8]

---

8. At the most fully aggregated level—that is, with the government and the private sector consolidated—there would be no meaningful distinction between the demand and supply

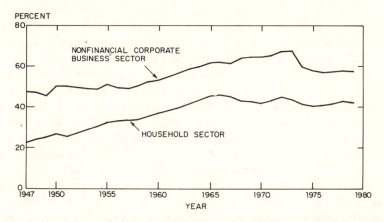

Fig. 6.3   Liabilities as a Percentage of Tangible Asset Holdings

The most interesting implications of the resulting "asset demand" hypothesis concern the role of equities in asset holders' portfolios, and the nature of financial intermediation. Because what is stable in relation to income is outstanding *debt* liabilities of nonfinancial borrowers, a stable demand for total financial assets is, in the end, not a sufficient explanation after all. In addition, it is necessary to posit not only that investors treat debt and equity securities as only weakly substitutable— an assumption that in turn bears importantly on the debate about the "ex post crowding out" of private spending by debt-financed fiscal policy— but also that, in holding debt obligations issued by an intermediary, investors look through the shell of the intermediary too.[9]

Test Results.   Efforts thus far to test these three potential explanations for the stable debt-to-income relationship, using data for the U.S. household and nonfinancial corporate business sectors, have not produced conclusive results.

Perhaps the strongest statement possible on the basis of these results is that the capital-leveraging hypothesis is clearly not the *entire* answer. As Figure 6.3 shows, neither individuals nor nonfinancial business corporations have on balance increased their indebtedness merely in pace with their ownership of tangible assets. During 1947–66 for individuals, and during 1957–73 for corporations, the rapid increase in private sector indebtedness also represented increasing leverage.

side of the asset markets for purposes of measurement. This problem is merely an example of the fundamental identification problem emphasized by Brainard and Tobin (1968) and Smith (1975).

9. My earlier paper (Friedman 1978) showed why the substitutability of debt and equity securities is so important for the "crowding out" issue.

Tests do, however, reveal at least some positive evidence consistent with each of the three hypotheses (see Friedman 1981). For example, the dynamic relationship between the federal and nonfederal components of the total nonfinancial debt-to-income ratio shows a distinct tendency for the nonfederal debt ratio to fall in relation to a positive innovation (in the sense described in Section 6.2) in the federal debt ratio, after a delay of about one year. Conversely, a positive innovation in the nonfederal debt ratio causes the federal debt ratio to fall, essentially without delay. In a study of the three-way interaction among federal debt, corporate debt, and corporate tangible asset holdings, a positive innovation in the federal debt ratio immediately reduces corporate tangible assets and corporate indebtedness relative to income, thereby lending support to the capital-leveraging hypothesis. In an analogous study for the household sector, a positive innovation in the federal debt ratio immediately reduces household tangible assets relative to income, but the associated reduction of household indebtedness follows only after a puzzling delay of two years.

Overall, although (at least) three different explanations are available for the observed stability of the debt-to-income relationship in the United States, the evidence now at hand is insufficient to choose among them. The debt-to-income phenomenon remains for the present a major puzzle. In light of its potential importance, finding the right explanation is an objective that clearly warrants further research.

6.4   Implications for Debt and Equity Financing of Capital Formation

An increased rate of capital formation has emerged as a nearly undisputed objective of U.S. economic policy for the 1980s. Dissatisfaction with the U.S. economy's poor productivity performance in the 1970s, as well as with the erosion of international competitiveness that began much earlier but also became more evident in the 1970s as the international exchange value of the dollar declined dramatically, has elevated what was once largely a business interest into a much more widely shared goal. In today's environment, groups representing labor and consumers also recognize the need for capital investment to create jobs and to raise productivity and hence the population's overall standard of living. On the whole, public discussion has moved from whether more capital formation is desirable to what policies can best achieve it.

An important aspect of capital formation that this discussion has often overlooked, however, is its explicitly financial side. In an economy like that of the United States, each decision to create more physical capital necessarily has a financial counterpart. Moreover, the financial transactions associated with capital formation are not merely a reflection of real resource allocations that would necessarily come about in any case. The

Table 6.4   Financing of U.S. Investment in Plant and Equipment

	Investment in Plant and Equipment, as Percentage of Gross National Product		Nonfinancial Corporate Business Sources of Funds, as Percentage of Total Sources		Nonfinancial Corporate Business Sources of External Funds, as Percentage of Total Sources		
	Gross Investment	Net Investment	Internal Funds	External Funds	Equity	All Debt	Short-Term Debt
1956–60	9.8%	2.6%	68.8%	31.2%	4.4%	26.8%	6.8%
1961–65	9.4	2.9	66.4	33.6	1.0	32.6	7.7
1966–70	10.6	4.0	58.4	41.6	2.3	39.3	10.6
1971–75	10.4	3.1	52.1	47.9	5.1	42.8	10.2
1976–80	11.0	2.8	56.9	43.1	2.1	41.0	12.9

SOURCE: U.S. Department of Commerce and Board of Governors of the Federal Reserve System.

setting in which the financing of capital formation takes place can also be a key determinant of real resource allocations, including not only the total amount of capital formation undertaken but also its composition. The financial and nonfinancial elements of the process jointly determine one another, and public policy can affect the ultimate outcome by influencing either.

It is also important to recognize that businesses and individuals in the U.S. economy have in fact been undertaking more capital formation rather than less, at least in the usual sense of investment in plant and equipment. As the first column of Table 6.4 shows, over the past quarter-century gross U.S. expenditures on plant and equipment have increased as a share of the nation's gross national product. More importantly, however, while *gross* capital formation has represented a progressively larger share of total output, the corresponding *net* capital formation underwent a sharp reversal within this period. As the second column of the table shows, net U.S. investment in plant and equipment (that is, net of the true economic depreciation) rose rapidly as a share of total output between the late 1950s and the late 1960s, but then fell back almost as rapidly by the late 1970s.

Still, it is gross capital outlays that the businesses and individuals investing in plant and equipment need to finance. Corporations engaged in nonfinancial lines of business have consistently accounted for nearly three-fourths of all U.S. investment in plant and equipment since World War II. As the next two columns of Table 6.4 show, over the last quarter-century the U.S. nonfinancial corporate business sector has increasingly relied on external as opposed to internal funds (including depreciation allowances) in financing its capital outlays.[10] Moreover, as the table's final columns show, corporations have consistently raised almost all of these external funds by issuing debt, and in doing so they have increasingly relied on short-term instruments (for further details see Friedman, forthcoming).

How has the economy absorbed this enormous expansion in the corporate sector's reliance on debt? As the discussion in Section 6.1 of the U.S. economy's stable overall debt-to-income ratio notes, the chief counterpart of the increasing corporate (and household) indebtedness relative to income over much of this period has been the federal government's declining indebtedness relative to income.

Recognition of this stable overall debt-to-income relationship raises two important questions about the financing of an increased rate of U.S. capital formation in the 1980s. First, if business corporations undertake sharply increased capital outlays, will they be able to continue their

10. The appearance of a reversal in the latest half-decade is largely due to the aftermath of the unusually severe 1973–75 recession as well as the 1980 recession.

reliance on debt financing if the federal government's indebtedness relative to gross national product declines only slowly (or not at all) as in the 1970s, in contrast to the rapid decline in the 1950s and '60s? The historical experience represented by the data shown in Table 6.1 and Figure 6.1 suggests otherwise. If the stability of the economy's aggregate nonfinancial debt-to-income ratio is indeed a regularity likely to persist, then the corporate sector will be able to undertake more investment in plant and equipment only if the government's relative indebtedness falls, or if corporations turn increasingly to equity finance through retention of internally generated funds or issues of new shares.

Second, even if declining federal government indebtedness relative to income does enable the corporate sector to finance increased capital outlays by further increasing its own indebtedness relative to income, what effect will this renewed change in the U.S. economy's government/private debt mix have on the economy's overall level of financial risk? In an economy with highly developed financial markets, potential hazards to the stability of the economy as a whole arise not just from the disruptions that from time to time may disturb the economy's nonfinancial activity directly but also from fragility of the financial superstructure built around it. Although a detailed consideration of the level of aggregate financial risk associated with any given further change in the government/private debt mix lies beyond the scope of this chapter, it is clear that, without a base of presumably default-free government debt (or private debt rendered default free through effective monetization), each market participant's financial assets consist simply of other market participants' liabilities.[11] Even if it is not necessary for the corporate sector to turn to equity finance because of an inability to increase its relative indebtedness, therefore, greater reliance on equity finance may nevertheless have an important role to play in the context of a sharply increased U.S. capital formation rate.

References

Brainard, William C., and Tobin, James. 1968. Pitfalls in Financial Model-Building. *American Economic Review* 57: 99–122.

David, Paul A., and Scadding, John L. 1974. Private Savings, Ultra-rationality, Aggregation, and "Denison's Law." *Journal of Political Economy* 82: 225–49.

11. Minsky's work has typically emphasized this issue; see, for example, Minsky (1972, 1977). My earlier paper (Friedman, forthcoming) discussed the resulting aspect of financial stability as a "public good."

Denison, Edward F. 1958. A Note on Private Saving. *Review of Economics and Statistics* 40: 261–67.

Friedman, Benjamin M. 1978. Crowding Out or Crowding In? Economic Consequences of Financing Government Deficits. *Brookings Papers on Economic Activity*, pp. 593–654.

———. 1980. Postwar Changes in American Financial Markets. In Feldstein, Martin, ed., *The American Economy in Transition*. Chicago: University of Chicago Press.

———. 1981. The Relative Stability of Money and Credit "Velocities" in the United States: Evidence and Some Speculations. National Bureau of Economic Research. Mimeographed.

———. Forthcoming. Financing Capital Formation in the 1980s: Issues for Public Policy. In Wachter, Michael L., and Wachter, Susan M., eds., *A New U.S. Industrial Policy*. Philadelphia: University of Pennsylvania Press.

Goldfeld, Stephen M., and Blinder, Alan S. 1972. Some Implications of Endogenous Stabilization Policy. *Brookings Papers on Economic Activity*, pp. 585–640.

Minsky, Hyman P. 1972. Financial Stability Revisited: The Economics of Disaster. *Reappraisal of the Federal Reserve Discount Mechanism*. Washington: Board of Governors of the Federal Reserve System.

———. 1977. A Theory of Systematic Fragility. In Altman, Edward, and Sametz, Arnold, eds., *Financial Crises: Institutions and Markets in a Fragile Environment*. New York: Wiley-International.

Modigliani, Franco. 1966. The Life Cycle Hypothesis of Saving, the Demand for Wealth and the Supply of Capital. *Social Research* 30: 160–217.

Modigliani, Franco, and Ando, Albert. 1976. Impacts of Fiscal Actions on Aggregate Income and the Monetarist Controversy: Theory and Evidence. In Stein, Jerome, ed., *Monetarism*. Amsterdam: North-Holland Publishing Company.

Sargent, Thomas J. 1976. The Observational Equivalence of Natural and Unnatural Rate Theories of Macroeconomics. *Journal of Political Economy* 84: 631–40.

Sims, Christopher A. 1980. Macroeconomics and Reality. *Econometrica* 48: 1–48.

Smith, Gary, 1975. Pitfalls in Financial Model Building: A Clarification. *American Economic Review* 45: 510–16.

List of Contributors

Zvi Bodie
School of Management
Boston University
Boston, MA 02215

John H. Ciccolo, Jr.
Department of Economics
Boston College
Chestnut Hill, MA 02167

Martin Feldstein
National Bureau of Economic Research
1050 Massachusetts Avenue
Cambridge, MA 02138

Benjamin M. Friedman
Department of Economics
Harvard University
Cambridge, MA 02138

Patric H. Hendershott
College of Administrative Science
Ohio State University
Columbus, OH 43210

Burton G. Malkiel
Yale School of Organization and Management
Yale University
New Haven, CT 06520

Index

DATE DUE

DEMCO 38-297